About Demos

Who we are

Demos is the think tank for everyday democracy. We believe everyone should be able to make personal choices in their daily lives that contribute to the common good. Our aim is to put this democratic idea into practice by working with organisations in ways that make them more effective and legitimate.

What we work on

We focus on six areas: public services; science and technology; cities and public space; people and communities; arts and culture; and global security.

Who we work with

Our partners include policy-makers, companies, public service providers and social entrepreneurs. Demos is not linked to any party but we work with politicians across political divides. Our international network – which extends across Eastern Europe, Scandinavia, Australia, Brazil, India and China – provides a global perspective and enables us to work across borders.

How we work

Demos knows the importance of learning from experience. We test and improve our ideas in practice by working with people who can make change happen. Our collaborative approach means that our partners share in the creation and ownership of new ideas.

What we offer

We analyse social and political change, which we connect to innovation and learning in organisations. We help our partners show thought leadership and respond to emerging policy challenges.

How we communicate

As an independent voice, we can create debates that lead to real change. We use the media, public events, workshops and publications to communicate our ideas. All our books can be downloaded free from the Demos website.

www.demos.co.uk

First published in 2007
© Demos
Some rights reserved – see copyright licence for details

ISBN 10 digit: 1 84180 177 1
ISBN 13 digit: 978 1 84180 177 3
Copy edited by Julie Pickard, London
Typeset by utimestwo, Collingtree, Northants
Printed by IPrint, Leicester

For further information and
subscription details please contact:

Demos
Magdalen House
136 Tooley Street
London SE1 2TU

telephone: 0845 458 5949
email: hello@demos.co.uk
web: www.demos.co.uk

Cultural Diplomacy

Kirsten Bound
Rachel Briggs
John Holden
Samuel Jones

DEM⊙S

Contents

Acknowledgements

We would like initially to thank the steering group for this project, whose support, advice and expertise was invaluable throughout the course of our work. In alphabetical order, they are: David Anderson, Leigh Gibson, Paul Howson, John Jackson, Ruth Jarratt, Joanna Mackle, Beth McKillop, Eimear Nic Lughadha, Oliver Urquhart Irvine, Jonathan Williams and Frances Windsor. Thanks also to Neil MacGregor whose initiative was instrumental in enabling the work to begin.

Conversations with Bruce Hellman have been useful throughout. His work on the International Strategy for the Department for Culture, Media and Sport (DCMS) has also been of immense value. Too numerous to mention, but always generous in their hospitality and comments are those whom we interviewed and who assisted us in China, Ethiopia, France, India, Norway and the United States. Similarly, in the UK, several people and organisations have been more than kind with their time, and thank you also to those who attended the two workshops we held during the course of the research. With regard to China, the expertise of Andrew Small was vital in setting up our trip, and the translations of Li Ke, not to mention her knowledge of Beijing, made our visits possible. During the research in India, and throughout the project, particular thanks to Shelagh Wright.

Thanks also to the Demos interns who helped support the project: Laura Bunt, Deena Chalabi, Yannick Harstein, Anni Oskala, Tracey Sartin and Abdus Shuman. Thanks also to Peter Harrington for his début in seeing the pamphlet through to publication. As always, our colleagues at Demos have been supportive and insightful in their comments. We wish to thank Catherine Fieschi and Mark Fuller in particular. All errors and omissions remain our own.

Kirsten Bound, Rachel Briggs,
John Holden and Samuel Jones
February 2007

Glossary

ACE	Arts Council England
ALVA	The Association of Leading Visitor Attractions
BBC	British Broadcasting Corporation
BC	The British Council
BL	The British Library
BM	The British Museum
BRIC	Brazil, Russia, India and China – the common reference term for the world's emerging powers
CBD	Convention on Biological Diversity
CCTV	China Central Television (the state broadcaster in the People's Republic of China)
DCLG	Department for Communities and Local Government
DCMS	Department for Culture, Media and Sport
Defra	Department for Environment, Food and Rural Affairs
DfID	Department for International Development
DTI	Department of Trade and Industry
EU	European Union
FCO	Foreign and Commonwealth Office
GSIF	Global Science and Innovation Forum
ICCR	The Indian Council for Cultural Relations
ICOM	The International Council of Museums

IFLA	The International Federation of Library Associations
IIT Bombay	The Indian Institute of Technology, Bombay
IMA	The International Music Association
IPNI	The International Plant Name Index
KFC	Kentucky Fried Chicken
LOCOG	London Organising Committee of the Olympic Games
The Met	The Metropolitan Museum of Art (New York)
MoMA	Museum of Modern Art (New York)
MoU	Memorandum of Understanding
NGA	National Gallery of Art (Washington, DC)
NHM	The Natural History Museum
NMDC	The National Museum Directors' Conference
ROH	The Royal Opera House
RSC	The Royal Shakespeare Company
UKTI	United Kingdom Trade and Industry
UN	The United Nations
Unesco	United Nations Educational, Scientific and Cultural Organization
USIA	US Information Agency, which conducted international educational and cultural exchanges, broadcasting and information programmes (folded into the State Department in 1999)
V&A	Victoria & Albert Museum

Executive summary

From the reciprocal gifts of ancient rulers to modern-day Expos, culture has been used as a way for leaders and countries to show who they are, assert their power and build lasting relationships. But in foreign policy, so often dominated by *realpolitik* thinking, culture and cultural exchange are often regarded as being desirable, but not essential. A common view is that, while cultural diplomacy can help establish and support working relationships between countries, it is strictly subordinate to the harder stuff of laws and treaties, bilateral negotiations, multilateral structures and military capability. While culture plays a role in diplomacy, there remains a stark contrast between the amount of attention, money and column inches devoted to this area, compared with more formal diplomacy.

Cultural Diplomacy argues that today, more than ever before, culture has a vital role to play in international relations. This stems from the wider, connective and human values that culture has: culture is both the means by which we come to understand others, and an aspect of life with innate worth that we enjoy and seek out. Cultural exchange gives us the chance to appreciate points of commonality and, where there are differences, to understand the motivations and humanity that underlie them. As identity politics exert an increasing influence on domestic and international exchanges, these attributes make culture a critical forum for negotiation and a medium of exchange in finding shared solutions. Cultural contact provides a forum for unofficial political relationship-building: it keeps open negotiating channels with countries where political connections are in jeopardy, and helps to recalibrate relationships for changing times with emerging powers such as India and China. In the future, alliances are just as likely to be forged along lines of cultural understanding as they are on economic or geographic ones.

The UK has a number of historical advantages in this regard. Our collections and performing companies are outstanding, we have highly skilled and respected cultural professionals, we are home to world-class artists, our culture and heritage act as magnets for tourism and business, and our creative industries are thriving. The UK boasts a strong tradition of international cultural exchange through the British Council's presence around the globe, and also via the dense global networks of our national cultural institutions and diaspora communities. From 2008, the eyes of the world will be on London as it begins its Olympiad ahead of the 2012 Olympic Games. This provides a unique and extended opportunity to showcase our cultural standing and to elaborate an understanding of the value of UK cultural diplomacy for a new era.

The UK cannot afford to rest on its cultural laurels. Investment in our cultural organisations and infrastructure must be on a par with that of the US and our European neighbours. We must create more mechanisms for engaging cultural institutions and professionals in the policy-making process so that we do not miss important opportunities. We must coordinate our efforts. Our research highlights a wealth of examples of good practice, but it suggests that the UK needs a more strategic and systematic approach to cultural diplomacy. In particular, with China and India placing increasing emphasis on culture in their approaches to cultural diplomacy, the UK must revisit its own attitudes and commitments to the power of this medium.

This report does not argue that culture should be used as a *tool* of public diplomacy. The value of cultural activity comes precisely from its independence, its freedom and the fact that it represents and connects people, rather than necessarily governments or policy positions. Highlighting a variety of national approaches to cultural diplomacy, this report exposes the universal challenge of finding an effective balance in the relationship between culture and politics.

The UK finds itself at an important crossroads. As we wrestle with the difficulties of relating to countries and communities in new ways, we must abandon old assumptions about the distinction between 'hard' and 'soft' power. Many of the challenges we face, such as climate change, terrorism and managing migration, cannot be solved by military might or unilateral policy innovations. Cultural diplomacy has a critical role to play. The ability to mobilise cultural diplomacy is a precious resource in international relations, and not one that rests only in the hands of our diplomats: we all need and have a duty to realise its potential. In the twenty-first century, it will be the countries that manage to make hard and soft power work together, hand-in-hand, that will succeed in achieving their goals.

Cultural Diplomacy sets out an ambitious programme for change, with recommendations for the UK government, the British Council and cultural institutions, which are outlined below and at greater length in the main body of the text. The report's recommendations are divided into five broad areas:

O   *Effective governance systems*: recommendations include the formation of a broad stakeholder Cultural Diplomacy Working Group run by the Public Diplomacy Group at the Foreign and Commonwealth Office.

O   *Political leadership*: recommendations are built around the critical need to invest in maintenance of the UK's global cultural standing and the need to capitalise on the expertise of cultural professionals in policy-making.

O   *The Olympic offering*: recommendations include the creation of a group of cultural ambassadors for the Olympic Games and making cultural diplomacy a central theme of a cross-government public diplomacy strategy for 2012.

O   *Cultural literacy*: we make a number of recommendations designed to ensure that the next generation of Britons will be equipped with the skills of cultural literacy needed to deal with challenges faced in a new era of global relations. The report also suggests ways in which diaspora communities can play a greater role in foreign policy.

○ *New technological challenges*: the report recommends that new technologies be the basis for innovative new working strategies rather than tacked on to old ones. Online strategies should reflect the full range of possible contributions to cultural diplomacy.

Introduction

In the long course of history, having people understand your thought is much greater security than another submarine.

J William Fulbright

Cultural exchange has been intertwined with the pursuit of foreign relations throughout history. From the reciprocal gifts of arts and manufactures between the Doge of Venice and Kublai Khan, to the Great Exhibition of 1851, to the present day, people have used culture to display themselves, to assert their power, and to understand others. Thomas Jefferson's letter to James Madison, sent from Paris in 1785, still provides a useful summary of the motivations that underpin cultural diplomacy: 'I am an enthusiast on the subject of the arts. But it is an enthusiasm of which I am not ashamed, as its object is to improve the taste of my countrymen, to increase their reputation, to reconcile to them the respect of the world and procure them its praise.' Fast-forward 200 years and nothing has changed. As Fulbright's quote reminds us, cultural relations remain central to international affairs.

We can, then, think of cultural diplomacy as one facet of international relations, as one of the 'soft' aspects of living together on the planet, rather than the 'hard' stuff of laws and treaties, multilateral organisations and military capability. The former US Secretary of State, Donald Rumsfeld, said that he did not understand the concept of 'soft power',[1] but security expert Walter Laqueur, sees it differently: 'Cultural diplomacy, in the widest sense, has increased in importance, whereas traditional diplomacy and military power . . . are of limited use.'[2]

The term 'cultural diplomacy' is not easily defined. When thinking about culture, we have taken as our starting point the United Nations' 1948 Universal Declaration of Human Rights, in which Article 27(1) states that: 'Everyone has the right freely to participate in the cultural life of the community, to enjoy the arts, and to share in scientific advancement and its benefits.' In this report, we take a broad view of what the term culture includes, and discuss science, sport and popular culture as well as the performing and visual arts and heritage. In our research, we have been working primarily with partners among the 'memory institutions' (the British Library, British Museum, Natural History Museum and Victoria & Albert Museum), the scientific/cultural institutions (Royal Botanic Gardens, Kew, and Natural History Museum), in the performing arts with the Royal Opera House, and with the cultural agency the British Council (BC), which undertakes cultural relations activities on behalf of the Foreign and Commonwealth Office (FCO).

In addition to extensive research in the UK, we have carried out fieldwork in China, Ethiopia, France, India, Norway and the United States of America and undertaken detailed desk research on Iran. The differences in national approaches are summarised in the appendix. Our aim has been to understand how different nations approach and carry out their cultural diplomacy in order to make recommendations about how the UK should develop its strategy, policy and practices in this area.

One significant finding is that it is becoming more important for us to pay attention to cultural diplomacy. We are moving from a world where the term was primarily concerned with relations between elites – where static and traditional cultural settings provided the opportunity and backdrop for relaxed ambassadorial and political contact, for example – to one where culture is also a medium between people on a mass scale. Many-to-many cultural exchange is now very fast moving and capable of profound effect, both laterally and upwardly, to the extent that cultural diplomacy now directly affects and may even direct the more traditional forms of public diplomacy.

Cultural diplomacy has also gained in significance as the world has moved from the bi-polarity of the Cold War to the uncertainties of the present multi-polar world. This has had a profound impact on the ways in which nations construct and project their national identity. Cultural, religious and ethnic factors now play a larger part in defining our sense of self and community. The emerging Asian powers understand the importance of culture and are consciously using it as a means to project themselves not just to foreign governments, but also to global public opinion and potential partners and allies. In doing so, they are offering different economic and political models to compete with those of the West.

The growing importance of cultural diplomacy *now*, together with the broader concept of public diplomacy, is reflected in a number of recent developments. In the space of the last 12 months, DCMS published its International Strategy, the Carter review of public diplomacy led to the establishment of the Public Diplomacy Board, and the FCO clarified its foreign policy priorities in a white paper.[3] These high-level developments have been reflected at operational level. United Kingdom Trade and Industry (UKTI), for example, published a strategy for the performing arts, including the formation of the Performing Arts International Development group, while Arts Council England (ACE) recently added 'international' to its list of priorities, pledging to 'promote our artists internationally, encourage international exchange and co-production, and do all we can to ensure that audiences and artists in this country benefit from the best of the arts from outside the UK'.[4] These initiatives, taken as a whole, show how cultural diplomacy is being taken ever more seriously, although, as this report argues, we have yet to organise ourselves in a way that meets the scale of change taking place.

Alongside this increased policy interest, there are examples of where we are getting things right in practice, demonstrating that sustained investment and proper coordination work. The British Museum's (BM's) Africa Programme, for example, began in 2003 as a three-year DCMS-funded initiative with equal in-kind support from the British Council. DCMS agreed to continue seed-corn money for two further years, allowing the initiative to leverage major funds from a private foundation. This successful multi-partner programme involves a series of events, exhibitions, debates and training initiatives in the UK and nine African countries. A total of 20 African countries are reached when collaboration with a transnational non-governmental organisation in West Africa is taken into account. It is operationally effective and entirely congruent with long-term diplomatic and development goals.[5] Similarly, 'China–UK: Connections through Culture' is a £1 million initiative funded by DCMS, FCO, the British Council and Scottish Executive that 'helps cultural organisations in both countries build and sustain strong relationships with each other, leading to increased exchange of cultural product between China and the United Kingdom'.[6] These are examples of synergy, and there are others in everyday practice not linked to high-profile programmes, such as when British Council language and education work takes place alongside exhibitions, education and capacity-building.

But we need to be doing more. British cultural organisations play a vital role in cultural and foreign relations; however, much that they do is not specifically funded, there is little coordination, and there are few information resources on which they can draw. The UK's cultural standing is materially important, both economically and in terms of international political influence, but this does not appear to be appreciated across the whole of government. We are under-investing in our cultural institutions, there are few formal mechanisms for engaging these organisations and other cultural leaders in the policy-making process, and there are many examples of missed opportunities. Our competitors are playing a much more strategic game, and we need to match or exceed their efforts if we are not to be left behind.

Cultural diplomacy, which is about the quest for the tourist dollar as well as the battle for hearts and minds, is a competitive marketplace. The UK has lost its primacy in manufacturing, sport and politics, but is still among world leaders in terms of culture. The breadth of its cultural contact with the rest of the world is huge, ranging from the big national institutions to small regional and amateur organisations. Within this, the national institutions occupy a special place in terms of their profile, scale, activity and mandate. However, as this pamphlet shows, their position as global leaders is constantly under pressure, and cannot be taken for granted. To be effective, the UK's cultural status – in terms of material assets and professional capacity – must be vigilantly maintained and kept up to date.

Culture is a major determinant of how people perceive each other and negotiate their differences. Opportunities for global contact and exchange are proliferating as never before, and because of those contacts, culture itself is changing. No longer can we think of relatively static cultures presenting themselves to each other for understanding and appraisal. Instead, cultures are meeting, mingling and morphing.

This presents governments and cultural organisations with a dual challenge: on the one hand they need to maintain established standards of scholarship, quality and continuity in the face of proliferating content and international competition, and on the other, to enable mass populations to develop the vital skills of cultural literacy – where people are able to understand themselves, and others, and the dynamic relationship between the two. In a world where popular culture can generate instant discord, there is an ever greater need for the formal cultural sector to continue its role of mediation and explanation: cultural chasms are best dealt with by building cultural bridges.

This report sets out an ambitious agenda for change with recommendations for the British government, British Council and the major cultural institutions that cover five broad areas: building effective governance systems, developing political leadership, using the Olympics as a focus for partnership working, cultural literacy, and responding to the challenges and opportunities posed by new technologies.

In an increasingly interconnected world, we should no longer think of culture as *subordinate to* politics. Instead we should think of culture as *providing the operating context for* politics.

1. Culture is an essential component of international relations

In the autumn of 1526, a young man stepped off a boat and onto the streets of London in search of a career. He was destined for the court of the English king, Henry VIII, helping the image-conscious monarch to assert his position as one of Europe's most important and respected rulers of the day. The man was Hans Holbein, who went on to produce work of the 'quality that would ensure the English king could hold his head high among his European rivals'.[7]

Great artists have always been a key asset to any leader. Rubens was both court artist and official ambassador. The films of Leni Riefenstahl and the architecture of Albert Speer were put at the service of the German Nazi regime in the 1930s. The Cold War relied heavily on cultural and scientific proxy battles between East and West in the form of the Bolshoi Ballet, Abstract Expressionism and the space race.

Diplomats use culture in many different ways. A collection of seventeenth- and eighteenth-century watches and clocks in the Palace Museum in Beijing highlights some of the impacts that can be achieved. The collection contains prestigious British clocks and watches given to China by visiting emissaries. It is one of China's choicest foreign collections and is visited by cultural professionals from the West,[8] including scholars from the British Museum who have documented and studied it in great detail. Initially, the clocks and watches were intended to impress Chinese dignitaries who had shown a fascination with automata.[9] But these clocks also demonstrated British manufacturing prowess and were symbolic of British values: its culture of innovation and precision, and its mastery over Nature and Time. The clocks – just like paintings, films and scientific endeavour – communicate values and speak to people in ways that are more subtle and less intrusive than direct propaganda.

Despite the ubiquity of culture in international relations, its importance is not well recognised. As later chapters will show, culture delivers tangible benefits in a number of different settings, but in the UK and elsewhere it continues to be perceived as an add-on, rather than being part of the core business of foreign relations. As international relations scholar Rajan Menon comments: 'Few Americans appreciate the degree to which knowledge about American culture, whether acquired by participating in our exchange programmes, attending our cultural presentations, or simply listening to the Voice of America, contributed to the death of communism.'[10] The UK has had a commitment to international cultural relations for many decades, perhaps best exemplified by the fact that the British Council has been funded by the FCO since 1934. This continuous commitment recognises that lasting relationships are built through long-term engagements, and other countries too have organisations with similar aims, from Germany's Goethe Institutes to China's recently established Confucius Institutes. But sometimes the short term wins. As Ed Mortimer, former Head of Communications at the UN, told us: 'This longer burn stuff almost has to be forced upon us.'[11]

The rise of public diplomacy: from few-to-few to few-to-many

There has been a growing recognition in recent years of the importance of influencing foreign citizens, as well as their leaders. Where diplomacy – 'the art or practice of conducting international relations, as in negotiating alliances, treaties and agreements'[12] – focuses on conversations and relationships between a small number of elites, public diplomacy aims to reach the masses. Although public diplomacy and cultural diplomacy are distinct phenomena, they cannot be totally separated from one another.

There is, however, no consensus about the aims and methods of public diplomacy. Inherent within all public diplomacy work is the Harvard Professor of International Relations, Joseph Nye's, idea of soft power.[13] While hard power is the ability to coerce (through military or economic means), soft power is the means to attract and persuade. As one British expert has put it: 'Public diplomacy is based on the premise that the image and reputation of a country are public goods which can create either an enabling or disabling environment for individual transactions.'[14]

Different countries develop models of public diplomacy suited to their global outlook, capacity and pre-existing profile. These extend from the Norwegian 'niche' approach that concentrates on the delivery of a limited number of simple messages, to the arm's length, distributed system of the UK, and from the centralised and state-funded French approach, to the news management or even 'propaganda' model of the US and China. Approaches also differ over time as local, national, regional and global dynamics change.

The appendix summarises the main differences in national approaches.

UK approaches to public diplomacy

In the UK, the 2006 Carter Review introduced a new definition of public diplomacy: 'work aiming to inform and engage individuals and organisations overseas, in order to improve understanding of and influence for the United Kingdom in a manner consistent with governmental medium and long-term goals'.[15] The review marked an important shift in approaches in the UK, because it moved away from the idea that public diplomacy aims merely to change *perceptions*, to the notion that it should also seek to change *behaviour*, in line with the government's international priorities.

There are a number of principles that underpin UK approaches to public diplomacy. In an article for *Foreign Policy* in 2002,[16] Mark

Leonard outlined the four purposes for public diplomacy in the twenty-first century:

O *increasing familiarity* – making people think about your country and updating their image of it

O *increasing appreciation* – creating positive perceptions of your country and getting others to see issues from your perspective

O *engaging people* – encouraging people to see your country as an attractive destination for tourism and study and encouraging them to buy its products and subscribe to its values

O *influencing people's behaviour* – getting companies to invest, encouraging public support for your country's positions, and convincing politicians to turn to it as an ally.

In order to achieve these goals, he argued that public diplomacy needs to operate in three dimensions – and that all three must be covered for the overall strategy to be effective. First, governments need to deal with *communication on day-to-day issues*, which requires them to align themselves with the news agenda. In particular, they must stop distinguishing between foreign news stories and domestic ones as if the audiences were entirely different. Second, they need to use *strategic communication* to manage the overall perceptions of their country. Strategic communication is made problematic by the fact that different institutions are responsible for managing different aspects such as politics, trade, tourism, investment and cultural relations. Third, governments must *develop lasting relationships* with key individuals through scholarships, exchanges, training, seminars, conferences and access to media channels. These relationships are not built between diplomats and people abroad, but between peers (politicians, special advisers, business people, cultural leaders and academics).

Cultural activity has an important contribution to make to public diplomacy in terms of both strategic communication and relationship building, but, as this report shows, it is currently undervalued by government and poorly coordinated. Opportunities are missed: for example, while the DCMS has pledged to 'make Britain the world's creative hub', there was no means of joining up concurrent exhibitions in 2006 of Zaha Hadid's architectural designs (at the Guggenheim) and British fashion design (at the Metropolitan Museum of Art) (the Met), on either side of New York's Fifth Avenue. Both exhibitions spoke for themselves, but they also provided a potential context for further, constructive activity.

Moreover, a number of emerging trends in global relations and communication suggest that culture could become the most important tool for public diplomacy practitioners, making its effective use vital. British public diplomacy will increasingly need to have culture at its heart.

The rise of non-state actors

The assumption that public diplomacy is the sole preserve of the state has increasingly been brought into question. It has had to adapt to the changing technological, social and political landscape. Public diplomacy's trinity of activities – news management, strategic communication and relationship building – emphasise long-term activities designed to open up one country to another, rather than project an image or message for immediate consumption. In an age of political cynicism, where politicians are generally held in low esteem by their electorates and where anti-Westernism is rife, public diplomacy cannot be purely an exercise in messaging. As Paul de Quincey, director of British Council Paris, commented, 'Rather than pushing a message out . . . you can't tell people how good you are; you have to show them.'[17]

Public diplomacy expert Jian Wang put it this way: 'With worldwide proliferation of media technologies and facile and affordable information access, the credibility and efficacy of the national government, as the primary communicator, are now often suspect.'[18] He suggests that there are three levels of public diplomacy activity, each of which requires the involvement of a different configuration of actors: promoting a country's national goals and policies (primarily national actors); communicating a nation's ideas and ideals, beliefs and values (national and sub-national actors); and building common understanding and relationships (primarily sub-national actors).

Culture operates on all three levels. In the 1950s, US values were communicated through the individual art of Jackson Pollock (indeed its individuality was part of its diplomatic value), as much as through the rhetoric of the State Department. Today the US singer Toni Blackman is the US's 'Hip-Hop Ambassador' and ice skater Michelle Kwan has been appointed as an official 'American Public Diplomacy Envoy'. In the 1990s, music, art and fashion were all central to the global presentation of 'Cool Britannia'.

It is through culture that we find points of commonality and difference, and the means to understand one another. Exhibitions, performances and other cultural forms enable us to engage with others' heritage and living culture. Outside Washington's National Gallery, the Smithsonian Folklife festival provides visitors with experiences of different cultures, exemplified by musicians from Castro's Cuba giving the US public a taste of the clubs and bars of Havana. That experience offered a contrast to more hostile images of Cuba that are common in the US media. Indeed, one of the most important contributions that culture can make to a country's public diplomacy is its ability to showcase a diversity of views, perspectives and opinions, breaking down persistent national stereotypes and challenging the perception that a country's political leaders and their policies are identical with the views of their citizens. This is particularly important when a country suffers reputational damage, such as that currently being experienced by the US and UK following the invasion of Iraq in 2003.

The US provides a good illustration. Its response to unpopularity has been to assume that its position would improve if foreigners understood its policies better. This ignores the fact that many aspects of not just American government policy but also American values are deeply unpopular. This cannot be simplistically reduced to the idea of a clash of civilisations; there are real misgivings about certain aspects of the 'American Dream'. As Wolf and Rosen have said:

> *Among some groups, cultures, and subcultures, American values and institutions are already reasonably well understood yet intensely resisted and disliked. Misunderstanding of American values is not the principal source of anti-Americanism. The source lies in explicit rejection of some of the salient characteristics of American values and institutions. Women's rights, open and competitive markets, and equal and secret voting rights – let alone materialism and conspicuous display – are (in some places and for some groups) resented, rejected, and bitterly opposed.*[19]

Culture provides meeting points for exposition and explanation, for dialogue and debate. In the case of the UK, these cultural spaces are given greater significance due to the high regard in which our national institutions are held. The reasons why UK cultural institutions are held in such esteem are explained in chapter 3, but it is important to recognise that their reputation is maintained only by constant vigilance and continual renegotiation. Our national cultural institutions are not static depositories for cultural artefacts; they are active participants in the articulation and communication of our own and others' sense of identity. Museums, galleries and libraries in particular 'provide the means by which a nation represents its relationship to its own history and to that of "other" cultures, functioning as monuments to the nation, and as such they have played a pivotal role in the formation of nation states'.[20]

At the same time, music and the performing arts can convey images of creativity, vitality and vibrancy. Throughout the Cold War, the Bolshoi and Kirov ballets presented a more approachable face of the USSR, and, today, Brazil is known far more for its carnival than its politics.

Aside from their de facto 'representation' of the UK overseas, cultural institutions regularly promote and showcase national interests. The Royal Academy, for instance, has collaborated with the British Council on architectural exhibitions in China and Japan, which relate closely to the government's focus on creativity. Likewise, the The Natural History Museum's (NHM's) Darwin Centre has become an international showcase for UK science, both physically and virtually, and thereby contributes to the agendas of the DCMS, the Department of Trade and Industry (DTI) and the Department for Environment, Food and Rural Affairs (Defra). International exhibitions, known as Expos, provide particular moments for showcasing British culture, art and science, and the 2005 Aichi Expo in Japan provides a useful example, visited by millions of people.[21]

Other activities can help to seize the moment at key points for bilateral exchange. The 1991 exhibition *Visions of Japan*, mounted by the Victoria & Albert Museum (V&A) during the UK's Japan Festival, was important in opening contemporary Japan to the UK public at a time when commercial, political and economic relations were growing in intensity.

In the white paper *Active Diplomacy for a Changing World*, published in March 2006, the FCO outlined ten strategic priorities for the UK.[22] The contribution of culture to these aims is dealt with implicitly and explicitly throughout this report (for example the contribution to the economy in chapter 2), but the real world impacts of culture are not always recognised. This is in part why culture's role in international affairs is consistently underestimated.

The reach of culture

Culture has the ability to reach substantial numbers of people, making it an ideal medium for public diplomacy. 'Culture' has a broad definition. Both the established institutions of culture and contemporary art and performance exist within, and interact with, a wider context of popular culture. Efforts on the part of cultural institutions to grow their audiences, coupled with new approaches to display, performance, interpretation and digitisation, mean that the distinction between 'high' and 'popular' culture seems increasingly outmoded. For example, in 2003 the BM's exhibition *The Treasure of the World's Cultures* attracted 1.3 million visitors on its tour to four Japanese cities and a further 600,000 across South Korea, before travelling to Beijing in 2006. Each year the British Library's (BL's) website generates some 24 million hits and the British Council facilitates over 1500 cultural events in 109 countries that are not one-off engagements, but part of long-term projects, programmes and relationships. These are big numbers, but it is not only exhibitions and performances that have mass appeal and effects. Education work can reach a lot of people too: the British Library's International Dunhuang Project is providing learning materials to thousands of Chinese school children. Similarly, performances have extensive reach; they are not confined to the theatre or concert hall, but are broadcast through the mass media of radio, television and the internet.

Mass popular culture has a global reach. This is not a new phenomenon – Hollywood has been providing points of common reference for a century – but it is changing in scale, speed and effect. Franchised television programmes, such as *Who Wants to be a Millionaire?* and *The Weakest Link* are becoming shared cultural forms; exported programmes like *Friends*, *Coronation Street* or *Sex and the City* are windows onto life somewhere else; and pop music mixes and mingles blues, bhangra and reggae in a riot of hybridity.

Food is another important cultural export. Recognising the importance of its cuisine, Thailand has used restaurants overseas as a means of promoting its culture and tourism. In 2003, the government launched 'Global Thai', a plan to boost the number of Thai restaurants around the world in a bid to drive tourism and promote awareness of Thailand.[23] The popularity of the first McDonald's restaurant in the former USSR in the late 1980s sent a potent message of popular rejection of the Soviet model. Kentucky Fried Chicken (KFC) is China's favourite brand,[24] and today, the dominance of western brands in places like China and India is brought into acute focus by the presence of a Starbucks in Beijing's Forbidden City – a presence that is now the focus of a cultural battle of its own.[25]

Another factor affecting mass cultural exchange and interaction is the step change that has occurred in the use of the internet. The emergence of YouTube,[26] where every day millions of people watch over 70 million videos, and other social websites like Bebo and MySpace have generated a more participatory form of globalised culture. Social software has multiplied spaces for, and forms of, cultural communication, creating a multitude of points of connection that do not respect borders or conventional definitions of nations.

Popular culture offers a starting point that increases cultural visibility and can sometimes help to open doors. That helps to explain why Czech president Vaclav Havel – himself a writer – suggested that Frank Zappa act as his 'Special Ambassador to the West on Trade, Culture and Tourism', why Ken Livingstone took pop group Girls Aloud with him on a recent trip to China, and why David Beckham was so important to London's bid for the 2012 Olympic Games. Case study 1 of Wyclef Jean in Haiti provides a similar example.

Case study 1: Wyclef Jean

Wyclef Jean, former member of the band the Fugees and now a solo performer, was recently made a roving ambassador for his native Haiti. Speaking about the singer, Haiti's president, René Préval, described him as 'our best asset to promote the country's image around the world'.[27]

The move is designed to counteract the conventional picture of Haiti, a country scarred by violence and civil unrest and the poorest country in the northern hemisphere. Wyclef, who often wears the colours of the Haitian flag, has been constant in his support and promotion of his homeland and has started an aid foundation that uses 'the potent combination of music and development to create small-scale, manageable and replicable projects to contribute to Haiti's long-term progress'.[28] So successful and influential has Wyclef been, that his name has even been talked of in relation to the Haitian presidency.

Perhaps the most intriguing example of the impact of popular culture on public diplomacy comes from China. One of the FCO's main priorities for China relates to the desire for long-term political change (as seen in the FCO priority 'promoting sustainable development and poverty reduction underpinned by human rights, democracy, good governance and protection of the environment'). The format of the UK TV show *Pop Idol*, a talent contest for unsigned singers, was exported to China in 2005 under the name of *Supergirls* and has become a huge success. Most significantly, it has introduced the concept of voting to a country that has never held national elections.

The grand finale was viewed by 400 million, mostly young, Chinese viewers who could vote via text message – although the word 'vote' was avoided. In 2005, eight million did so, and the winner, Li Yuchun – the subject of many a chat-room discussion – attracted 3.5 million messages. The success of *Supergirls* in China has raised some eyebrows. It was broadcast not by national TV, but by an independent production company from Hunan. An official statement from China Central TV (CCTV), the national state-run broadcaster, labelled it 'vulgar and manipulative' and criticised the gaudiness and impropriety of the girls' clothing. Beijing sociologist Li Yinhe, however, called it 'a victory of the grass-roots over the elite culture'.[29] Subsequently, Li Yuchun visited London at the mayor's invitation, performed outside City Hall, and drew a large crowd from the UK's Chinese community.

All these factors point towards two truths about the future of public diplomacy. First, that culture has an important role to play. And, second, that effective public diplomacy systems will be those that can cope with this new level of complexity and all the challenges that it throws up, from straightforward coordination, to the difficult business of judging the difference between engaging with culture and co-opting it for political ends. This will not be easy, but in later chapters we set out in detail a number of practical options that could allow the UK government to stay on the right side of that line.

2. Maximising the UK's cultural competitive advantage

The UK is a leading player in the cultural world. The strength of our historic collections, their global reputation, our long-term relationships with foreign institutions, the breadth and depth of expertise, and the creativity of the cultural sector together mean that the UK is at the forefront of thinking and practice on culture. However, at the start of the twenty-first century, and as new players and technologies come to dominate, there is a significant risk of the UK sitting on its cultural laurels and being overtaken by other countries, such as China and India, that understand the value of culture in public diplomacy and are committing significant resources to it. Overall, we are not coordinating our efforts effectively, nor are we spending enough on acquisitions to keep our collections up to date. There are insufficient incentives for the growing international work of our cultural institutions to be in tune with the UK's international priorities; there is little support for institutions hoping to work in harder-to-reach places. There is also danger that we will fail to realise the cultural diplomacy dividend offered by the 2012 Olympic Games and London's Olympiad, which begins in 2008.

The UK benefits from international cultural exchange

The UK's cultural sector produces direct and indirect economic benefits for the UK. Some of these benefits can be quantified, but many cannot, and this study does not attempt to calculate the overall economic windfall for the UK, a figure which would be highly approximate and the subject of intense debate and disagreement. The figures that are available paint a convincing picture of the value of culture to the British economy. First, culture generates income. The UK art and antiques market commands 25 per cent of global turnover and as long ago as 1999 amounted to £3.5 billion a year;[30] in 2002 the UK exported cultural goods to the value of £8.5 billion,[31] which included art production, performances, film, music and design; there is a growing market in the sale of advice, expertise and consultancy, ranging from conservation to sound engineering to policy; and the UK is a world leader in education and training relating to culture, ranging from higher education degree courses, to summer schools, to short courses, which take place both in the UK and overseas. Second, the UK's scientific collections provide the natural resources for scientific invention and medical advances. Third, the UK earns licensing revenue for goods and services that are not themselves classed as cultural, but which have a cultural component or inspiration. Examples include such things as pottery reproduced from archive designs, and furnishing fabrics inspired by textiles from public collections.

Tourism

Culture and heritage are primary drivers of international tourism. The UK receives 30 million overseas visitors each year, contributing £14.7 billion to our economy.[32] Museums account for seven of the top ten visitor attractions in the UK, and while there is no breakdown of these figures to show how this relates to international visitors, it would be reasonable to assume that the UK's rich cultural scene is an important pull factor for tourists. Figure 1 sets out the visitor numbers for various UK attractions in 2005. While London dominates this list, where theatre is also a particular tourist attraction, it would be wrong to assume that the tourism benefit is not felt outside the capital. Culture plays an important role in helping to spread the tourist pound around the entire country, from Dove Cottage in the Lake District and Shakespeare's Stratford, to the

Figure 1 2005 Vistor statistics

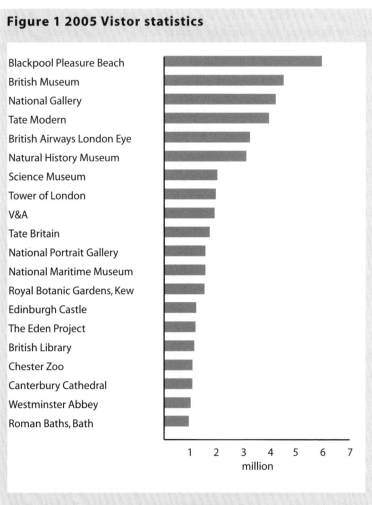

Source: Association of Leading Visitor Attractions, see
www.alva.org.uk/visitor_statistics/ (accessed 11 Feb 2007)

Edinburgh Festival and Tate St Ives. And the contemporary phenomenon of 'set-jetting', visiting film locations, has added to this trend: Alnwick's international tourist trade is no longer confined to fly-fishers and heritage devotees, but extends to Harry Potter enthusiasts, too.[33]

Tourism is important not just for its economic impact, but for the significance that it has in creating impressions about a country. The experience of a visit – how visitors are treated, what they see, hear and learn – will remain with them for years and be communicated to family and friends. In aggregate, these visitor impressions represent a powerful force in global political relations, colouring how a country's actions are perceived and giving it greater or lesser standing on the world stage. In this context, it is worth noting that the fastest growing group of overseas visitors to the UK is accounted for by the 'rest of the world' (ie not Europe or North America). This group, which includes China, India, Latin America and Russia, is growing at 18 per cent per year, with 6.5 million visits in 2005.[34]

With so many overseas visitors, the impressions created by our cultural institutions are of crucial importance. It is particularly vital that visitors see their own cultures being cared for and respected. The UK is home to many of the world's greatest treasures, and when someone travels halfway across the globe to see possibly the best exemplars of their own culture, she or he rightly expects the highest standards of access and interpretation and, increasingly, the opportunity to participate in creating new meaning for the object either by leaving comments, or otherwise adding opinion to the responses it garners.

But while the visitor numbers are impressive, it is essential to realise that international tourism is a competitive market, and when UK museums and galleries are looked at in terms of international comparators the picture looks less rosy. In 2005, out of the top-ranking 30 exhibitions globally in terms of attendance, the UK appears only twice – at nineteenth with Tate's *Turner Whistler Monet* exhibition, and at twenty-fifth with the Royal Academy's show *Turks*. The UK has not appeared in the top ten during the last three years.[35]

Again, these figures include both domestic and international visitors, but they do give a guide to the UK's standing. In France, the Louvre has experienced a huge increase in visitors over the last few years, from a total of about 6 million in 2000 to 7.5 million in 2005 and 8.3 million in 2006.[36] The number of Chinese visitors to the museum tripled in the 12 months prior to July 2006,[37] while the accession of Central and East European countries to the Europan Union (EU) has also significantly boosted its numbers. A virtuous circle exists: purposeful cultural diplomacy and investment encourages growth in tourism with consequent economic and reputational benefits that help justify further investment. **The FCO should collaborate with DCMS to monitor the number of tourists attracted by cultural institutions as a matter of course and use them as one of the proxy measures of the impact of the UK's public diplomacy work.**

As the UK gears up for London's Olympic Games and the start of the four-year Olympiad in 2008, these visitor figures should be weighing hard on the minds of the public diplomacy team at the FCO – of the huge number of people who will come to see the sport, most will also want to see UK culture. The Olympics offer an exciting and rare opportunity to showcase the UK's cultural credentials in front of both foreign visitors and a global television audience of billions. Culture, and an appeal to London's diversity, formed an important part of the UK's Olympic bid, and it is vital that the DCMS and the London Organising Committee of the Olympic Games' (LOCOG's) plans for the Cultural Olympiad are joined up with efforts by the FCO's Public Diplomacy Board. **We recommend that cultural diplomacy should be a central theme in the 2012 public diplomacy strategy in terms of both what the UK's cultural institutions and smaller organisations can do in the UK, and also how their overseas activities could feed into and complement the UK's agenda for the Games.**

Creativity

The creative industries (as defined by the DCMS[38]) form a fundamental part of the UK economy. The DCMS says that in 2004 the creative industries contributed 8 per cent to national gross value added, accounting for 20 per cent of jobs in London.[39] The relationship between this sector of the economy and the more strictly defined cultural sector is osmotic but unquantified. From the rock star Ian Brown getting his inspiration for a pop song from an exhibit at the NHM[40] to the filming of the National Theatre's *The History Boys*, from Royal Shakespeare Company (RSC)-trained actors doing Hollywood voiceovers, to advertising being inspired by contemporary art, there are numerous examples of crossovers. Britain's creativity is of great international interest: the V&A's tour of its Vivienne Westwood exhibition drew big crowds in Bangkok, Canberra, Düsseldorf, Shanghai, Taipei and Tokyo. All of these examples have an international dimension and an economic impact, generating export earnings for the UK.

But cultural institutions have more subtle effects as well. The UK's rich collections are an unrivalled storehouse for artists and designers. That is why the V&A, for example, is a vital resource for all design students, and why it attracts designers from Italy, Japan and elsewhere. Vivienne Westwood has spoken about the inspiration for her work that she finds in the Wallace Collection.[41]

The importance of cultural and creative exports is not only economic. As with tourism, there are issues of reputation and perception. Culture is one area where the UK is still a giant in global terms. British talent is world class in classical music, opera, pop music, theatre, literature and film acting. From Simon Rattle to Sam Mendes, from Razorlight to Jeremy Irons, notions of Britishness get conveyed to the rest of the world through personalities in a myriad of contexts. UK cultural talent can be found working all over the world; at least two of Chicago's cultural leaders – Tony Jones at the School of the Art Institute of Chicago and Sir Andrew Davis, Director of the Lyric Opera, are British. Likewise, leading figures from overseas practise their arts in the UK. The Cuban dancer Carlos Acosta is a principal at the Royal Ballet, for example. **In the UK's Olympic bid, we recognised the important role of cultural ambassadors. Government should be alive to finding more opportunities for** engaging cultural ambassadors in international relations, particularly where they are already resident abroad.

The economic and reputational benefits that the UK derives from culture are clear, but some of the other benefits of cultural activities are much less visible. One example of a powerful outcome – and one that contributed to the fulfilment of the UK's development goals – is a parasite eradication programme in Africa, funded by the United Nations to the tune of US$150 million. The programme was launched as a result of research undertaken at the NHM, and it has saved the lives of thousands of cattle in Africa. The consequent human and economic impact did not get captured in traditional ways of accounting for aid, and therefore has not been recognised as part of the UK's contribution to development. The benefits to the Department for International Development (DfID) from initiatives such as this are immense, and need to be understood and taken into account.

Culture is underpinned by a rich international network of structures, treaties, relationships and practices

The scale of activity that is undertaken by British cultural institutions overseas, alongside the work of the British Council, is vast. The DCMS mapping exercise of international activity, undertaken in 2006, concentrated on just 50 organisations, but showed that a great deal is happening on the ground. In fact, cultural activity taking place over decades has produced a network so rich that it rivals that of the official diplomatic network of the British government.

An international outlook is integral to the workings of most cultural institutions. The British Library calls itself 'a world memory organisation', holding 'the DNA of the world's civilisations'; the NHM is 'part of the global commons'; and the V&A is 'the world's leading museum of art and design'. The Royal Botanic Gardens, Kew, typifies the global reach and outlook of our major institutions. It works in over a hundred countries, with thousands of partners, creating and maintaining a wide variety of global resources including the International Plant Name Index (IPNI, in collaboration with Harvard University and the Centre for Plant Diversity Research, Canberra) and the Millennium Seed Bank. At the Royal Opera House (ROH), dancers and musicians come from all over the world and are ambassadors for each country where they were born or brought up.

The international work of cultural institutions is underpinned by systems of governance and self-governance, with one important informal instrument being the Memorandum of Understanding (MoU). These can exist between governments or institutions, and in many countries, the establishment of a MoU by a domestic cultural organisation with a foreign one will inextricably be bound up in politics, with an expectation of government-to-government contact. This means that, in practice, UK cultural institutions may sometimes need the cooperation of the FCO and local diplomatic contacts in order to establish MoUs. As highlighted by the case of the Louvre in Iran in the next chapter, such arrangements can help to maintain links between countries during times of political difficulty. **The FCO, in partnership with the cultural institutions, should carry out an assessment of the countries where official government-to-government MoUs would be beneficial, based on the UK's current international priorities**, with the BRIC countries (Brazil, Russia, India and China) being obvious contenders.

There are a number of other systems of governance that oversee different aspects of the work of cultural institutions. Unesco, which is part of the UN, is one of the most important. It acts as a clearing house, gathering and disseminating information, knowledge and best practices through research, publications, conferences and training; sets standards; builds capacity by helping with policy development, national strategies, projects, feasibility studies and raising funds; and acts as a catalyst for international cooperation. It is probably best known for its responsibility to designate World Heritage Sites, of which the UK currently has 27, including the Royal Botanic Gardens, Kew. World Heritage designation is an important driver not only of conservation, but of tourism, too.

International treaties also affect cultural institutions. In 1992, the Earth Summit was held in Rio, where world leaders agreed on a comprehensive strategy for sustainable development. A key element of this was the Convention on Biological Diversity (CBD), which was signed and ratified by the majority of the world's countries and within which institutions like the Natural History Museum and the Royal Botanic Gardens, Kew, play an important role in implementation and building best practice within the UK and worldwide.

There are also numerous organisations devoted to self-governance and cooperation, from the International Council of Museums (ICOM) to the International Federation of Library Associations (IFLA); from the International Music Association (IMA) to the Eurocities Culture Forum. These organisations variously encompass academic, commercial, professional and geographic interests, and form an important international confederacy. Many of their individual and/or organisational members are part of several groups, thus forming an overlapping set of relationships that promote flows of information, expertise and cooperation, and providing an obvious point of interface between the government and the cultural sector.

Our cultural institutions are good ambassadors for the UK

The UK's national cultural institutions work in the public interest. While there is, of course, healthy competition among them and between them and their peers overseas, their working model is underpinned by an understanding that their purpose is to serve the public interest. This is in turn how they earn their licence to operate, which then reinforces their public mandate. The public service nature of these institutions makes them effective, but unofficial, ambassadors for the UK while their public appeal makes them a valuable bridge between diplomacy, international relations and public opinion.

Through their collections and activities our national cultural institutions have an international responsibility and remit. As the National Museum Directors' Conference puts it: 'As institutions preserving, interpreting and presenting major cultural and national assets from around the world, we are by definition international in scope.'[42] For example, the NHM has many international collaborative research projects running each year, resulting in 500 peer-reviewed papers, about 80 per cent of which involve an overseas element. The V&A or Royal Botanic Gardens, Kew, could not fulfil their cultural and scientific functions without borrowing from, and lending to, overseas collections, and organising scholarly exchanges and visits. The BL cannot continue to fulfil its duties without continuing to acquire significant material – both by value and content – from overseas: in April 2006, it took the decision to give greater priority to the acquisition of Chinese material.[43] This inherent internationalism is not confined to the UK; in New York, one of the Museum of Modern Art's (MoMA's) curatorial directors told us: 'the Museum *is* international'. As a result, some cultural institutions are beginning to internationalise their governance structures to reflect their remit, character and operations. For example, more than half of the BM's trustees were born outside the UK.

The networks that have been developed by our cultural institutions are not restricted to other cultural institutions, but extend to government, scholarly peers and local communities. When Kew undertakes a plant collecting exercise or the BM undertakes an archaeological dig, their contacts will include everyone from the relevant authorising authorities in national and regional government to local manual workers and guides. Just as our opinions of other countries are shaped by personal experience, how our cultural organisations go about their business thus assumes significance in the way that the UK is perceived abroad by everyone from foreign ministers to workers. The effect of such contact can be even more powerful when it has an educational purpose. When the ROH carries out workshops in schools abroad, for example – as it has in China and South Africa – it can bring a whole new approach based on developing the creative potential of the individual. In countries where individual rights are neglected or even suppressed, this can provide a vital space for development.

The nature of their work also requires cultural institutions to be collaborative, not just because this is in the public interest, but because it makes their own work more effective and creative, too. For instance, when the V&A redesigned its Islamic galleries, the National Gallery of Art (NGA) in Washington asked to borrow some of the collections that were going to go into storage. The V&A obliged primarily as a matter of public service, but also in the knowledge that there would likely be opportunities in the future for the NGA to return the favour. There are a number of projects that involve multiple partners from different countries. The BL's International Dunhuang Project is a ground-breaking international collaboration to reunify cultural objects that are scattered around the world. This necessarily involves shared standards of curating, cataloguing, scholarship, technical issues and so on, but it will also result in making information and images of more than 100,000 manuscripts, paintings, textiles and artefacts from Silk Road sites freely available on the internet. Similarly, the NHM-led SYNTHESYS project involves 11 large collection institutions in creating a shared European infrastructure for research in natural science. The project is developing shared resources, common standards and funding access for scientists from 34 countries. Kew is at the heart of the African Plants Initiative enabling more than 50 institutions in Africa, Europe and the US to capture and share data for research and educational purposes.

As these examples show, cooperation is inherent to the way the institutions operate. Much of the NHM's international work is collaborative and specimens collected will be shared between the NHM, collaborators or museums in the country of origin, and sometimes museums in third countries. This agreed practice supports a distributed international system of collections, information and expertise that subsequently involves extensive sharing of collections and mobility of researchers. Furthermore, this openness is not reserved for other cultural professionals. Anyone from anywhere can walk into the NHM and have a specimen they have found identified. The museum gets tens of thousands of enquiries a year, and, while being generous with their expertise benefits the NHM itself and benefits science, it is also a notably open and democratic approach which is not written down or imposed on them. As one scientist from the NHM put it: 'British institutions are well respected as agenda-free, benign and professional and have power to influence the world in a gentle way. . . . It's partnership, collaborative, ad hoc, grassroots, not grand-planned, institutional.'

The UK has a duty of care

The UK's global standing carries with it heavy responsibilities for its collections and displays, in terms of conservation, access, scholarship and display, responsibilities that are in some cases heightened by the contested ownership of objects within the national collections. The UK's institutions are custodians of global resources, from material culture to plant specimens. They thus have a moral (as well as a legal) obligation to look after what they hold on behalf of source communities and of future generations, but they also have an obligation to make their collections as widely available as possible. Individually and collectively they have sought to do this by increasing physical access, touring objects widely, and by using new technology.

Maintaining the competitive advantage

Given the UK's world-class standing, it is surprising and worrying that culture does not receive more attention across government and that, as a nation, we are under-investing in our cultural infra-structure, as shown in figure 2, which outlines per capita spending for a number of European countries.

One of the most important areas of under-spend is on acquisitions. If our cultural institutions are to maintain the inspirational role that they have, we need to replenish and nurture them: cultural diplomacy cannot be sustained in the face of threatened funding cuts. Some of our institutions are unable to add contemporary work to their collections and repertory so cannot reflect the changing make-up of our own society, let alone maintain their position as an up-to-date global resource. The BL's drive to build its Chinese holdings is too isolated a case for a country that aims to be the 'world's creative hub'. The contrast with some of our international competitors is

Figure 2 Per capita spending on culture

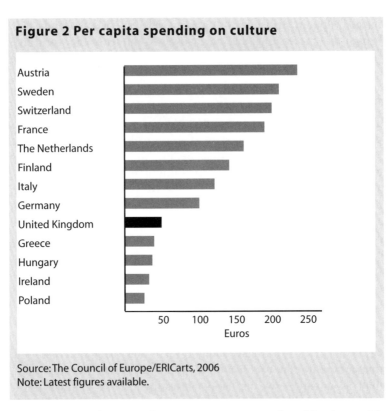

Source: The Council of Europe/ERICarts, 2006
Note: Latest figures available.

stark: in Egypt, for example, France supports a cultural institute with 30 archaeological digs and its own scholarly press; the UK has nothing approaching this level of investment.

The situation in the UK has become almost a national embarrassment, creating headline news in late 2006. The Art Fund published the results of a survey that compared the spending on acquisitions by major museums in four countries (see figure 3).[44] According to *The Art Newspaper*, 'the Metropolitan had more than eight times the purchasing power of the National Gallery, and a staggering 70 times the purchasing power of the British Museum; New York's Museum of Modern Art had four times the purchasing

Figure 3 Spending on acquisitions by major museums (2004/05)

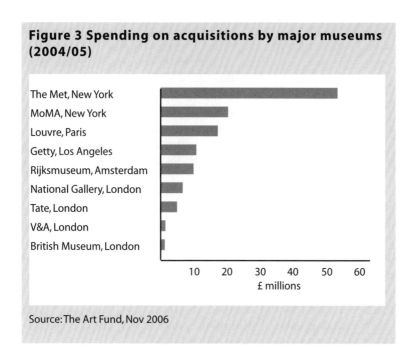

Source: The Art Fund, Nov 2006

power of Tate'.[45] While commentators are right to point out that figures can be skewed by major purchases of individual pieces, the point remains. **In a world in which cultural diplomacy will be ever more central, the UK must sustain its influence and credibility by support for acquisitions to maintain the range, quality and contemporary relevance of our cultural assets.**

But cultural diplomacy is not simply a question of funding. As the next chapter will show, it is vital that politicians appreciate the ways in which cultural settings offer opportunities for informal engagement and message-sending around diplomatic objectives. **Ministerial attendance at high-profile exhibition openings and premiere performances should be given greater priority by senior British politicians.** For example, at the opening of the Jameel Gallery at the V&A, attended by the Prince of Wales and Middle Eastern ambassadors, there was no high-level UK government presence, a missed opportunity at a time when engagement with the region has never been more important. Conversely, there are few instances of cultural professionals (other than those related to science) having a seat at the trade and policy table, the inclusion of the director of the British Museum as a member of the China Task Force being a notable exception. **Government departments should look for more opportunities to engage leading cultural professionals in the policy-making process, through their involvement in policy teams and commissions.**

The emerging powers are fast realising the importance of their own cultures and using them as one of their central tools of outward projection. Our government will take care of official ties, but if the foundations of broader cultural relationships are not in place, these will be fragile, especially as public opinion becomes ever more suspicious of government activity. We cannot afford to be complacent and expect our relative position of cultural strength to take care of itself. It is vital that the whole of government, in partnership with others including cultural institutions, works actively and energetically to maintain and strengthen our cultural standing.

Market forces often drive the international work of UK cultural institutions

Much of the work that the UK's cultural institutions do overseas is commercially driven. For example, not only has the NHM been touring exhibitions overseas commercially for 17 years, it has also provided consulting services to the European Union and the national museums of Kenya, Qatar and Dubai. The BL generates income from its publications and image supply, and the BM has advisory contracts in Kenya (funded by DCMS) and Qatar. These kinds of opportunities are particularly prevalent in the Gulf States, which see cultural tourism as a vital future component of their economies, and in Eastern Europe, where nations want to establish their identities, to restore their heritage, and to modernise their displays.

Touring exhibitions are a big business in their own right. The V&A

alone has over 20 exhibitions either on tour or in plan at any one time, and last year 700,000 overseas visitors saw V&A touring exhibitions in venues outside the UK. But touring and loans also involve cultural aims, such as encouraging reciprocity between UK and overseas institutions, and helping other countries to interpret their own histories through the loan of objects. One example of this happening in practice is the BM's *Hazina* exhibition in Kenya, where objects were lent to the National Museum in Nairobi, helping visitors to relate to cultures that permeate national boundaries, and to understand Kenya's neighbours. Another is the BM's loan of Assyrian objects to China. In these and other cases the UK's collections are being used to help multilateral relationships, not just the UK's own relationships.

The *Hazina* example shows how strategic investment pays off. Funded by the DCMS, one of its impacts has been to encourage private sector funders to support a sustainable BM programme in Africa.

While much of this work is highly worthwhile and adds value above and beyond the bottom line for the institutions themselves, it is surprising that there are few incentives for cultural institutions to coordinate their international work, where possible, with the international priorities of the UK. International cultural activity has not attracted the kind of cross-government structural experiments that exist in the sphere of science and education. For example, the DTI-led Global Science and Innovation Forum (GSIF) exists in part to generate leverage and influence, and a £25-million fund (the UK–India Education and Research Initiative) is being set up to promote collaboration in education and research between the UK and India. There is scope for these types of cross-government initiatives to be extended, and **the FCO and DTI should explore areas where similar opportunities could be opened up right across the cultural sector.**

The government should find ways to incentivise the work of our cultural institutions in the priority countries, such as Brazil, China and India. Currently, institutions have to follow the market: this is one reason why touring tends to be to the US which is relatively poor in collections terms, but cash-rich. At a time when the UK has prioritised engagement with the new emerging powers, such as China and India, and has dramatically stepped up funding for science in these countries, there has been no significant shift in funding or other support for institutions that want to expand their work in these countries. Major performing companies, like the Royal Ballet and the Royal Opera, for example, require substantial financial and other kinds of support to be able to tour and if the barriers to entry are too high they will not be able to work there.

We suggest that this kind of work be incentivised through three new activities. First, **the government should create a one-stop-shop assistance unit for British cultural institutions wishing to work outside the UK.** This would provide information about issues such as travel, visas and health; it could help to link British institutions with local partners in their destination countries; and it could provide information about potential funding sources. Second, **a modest fund should be created to support first-time collaboration by UK cultural institutions in priority countries.** This fund would help to build knowledge and capacity within the cultural sector about working in harder-to-reach countries. Often cultural institutions are not permitted to fund other institutions. The British Library recently provided a very large number of microfilms of Iraqi material for the Iraq National Library and Archive. This important diplomatic gesture would have been impossible without the modest £4500 provided by the FCO. There should be a mechanism through the one-stop-shop unit to share the growing body of information and best practice. And third, **the British Council should be supported to further promote collaboration between UK cultural institutions in priority countries.** We came across stories of British orchestras and other cultural professionals meeting by chance on the streets of cities like Beijing or Delhi, when they could have been collaborating to increase the overall impact and reach of their work.

For their part, **those cultural institutions that have not already done so should create international strategies, whose partial**

function would be to show how their international work contributes towards the UK's international priorities. The V&A and British Library, to take just two examples, have well-developed international policies that take account of articulated government priorities and include monitoring frameworks. Smaller organisations, such as touring theatre groups, often have no idea of FCO priorities, even when they are contributing to them. That is not to say that cultural or scholarly objectives should be driven by government's foreign policy agenda – that would not be in the UK's long-term interests and might give the impression that our institutions are political tools. However, for those institutions wishing to access the enhanced funding and services proposed in this report, they should be able to show how their work aligns with government priorities. **The creation and sharing of these documents would also help to develop a better understanding within government of what the cultural sector has to offer.**

One major unresolved issue that we came across in our research is that of visas. Visiting cultural professionals go through the usual visa procedures when they visit the UK and there have been instances when visas have been refused. This can be taken very badly. One interviewee expressed outrage that a UK institution could take the initiative by offering to host a visit, and then the person invited – a very high-ranking academic of seemingly unquestionable respectability – could be refused a visa. 'Where is the point in that?' he asked. The problem is that it is not unknown for high-ranking officials to disappear or to seek asylum once they are in the UK. One possible approach is that taken in the US, where a special category of visa exists to facilitate academic exchange.[46] This is a knotty problem, but we cannot ignore it and hope that it will go away; as international cultural exchange increases, the visa issue will become an even bigger thorn in the side of the UK.

It is important that we do not shy away from these difficult problems. There will be no easy solutions, but we must try various alternatives that might help to ease the situation. **The government should trial, for a limited period and under close observation, a**

new scheme for visa applications for people visiting the UK to conduct work of a cultural nature. The types of work would need to be carefully defined, and the individuals would need to provide references from their host cultural institutions in the UK, plus sufficient supporting information about their planned activities. This does not eradicate the risk of individuals abusing the system, but is a risk worth taking.

Even capacity-building is a competitive marketplace

Cultural tourism and cultural exports are competitive marketplaces, but so is the cultural battle for hearts and minds. Even the seemingly generous act of capacity-building is competitive: the BM's plan to assist in the development of an ethnographic open-air museum in Addis Ababa at the invitation of the Ethiopian government is marching in parallel with French assistance in refurbishing the National Museum, and US involvement in constructing a display on early human remains. Capacity-building is not only about creating good relationships. It also helps meet some of the UK's international obligations. For example, because of the UN Convention on Biological Diversity, it is essential to build capacities in developing countries in order to enable the implementation of the Convention in areas rich in biodiversity but ill-equipped to manage it effectively.

One example of the way that capacity-building works can be seen in the BM's relationship with Sudan. Here, the BM does fieldwork training, hosts Sudanese curators on a course in London, with follow-up in the country itself. Local capacity-building also includes learning through being involved in education work, exhibition design and display, advertising and marketing. In many countries where museum services are severely embattled and short of resources, all of this provides a big boost to morale. Building cultural capacity has beneficial knock-on effects: a better museum helps boost tourism, enhances a country's reputation, and plays a part in building civil society. But it also rebounds to the benefit of the western institutions. For example, the Metropolitan Museum in New York provides training for Chinese museum professionals in a scheme supported by the Andrew W Mellon Foundation – this is an important process because it creates an affiliation between the next generation of global museum leaders, thereby cementing the continuation of institutional relationships. The BM similarly runs a summer school for curators from all around the globe, and some places on it are supported by DCMS.

This chapter has shown just how important an asset culture is to the UK. In fact, culture is one area where the UK can still justifiably claim to be world class. Our museums, galleries and performances act as magnets for tourists and business investors alike; we are trading on a global scale in the art market and in television and publishing; and our cultural ambassadors are known the world over. But complacency in the global cultural market is dangerous: the US and our European neighbours are consistently investing more in their cultural stock. We need to understand how countries like China and India are making strategic use of culture in their global relationships, and, while the DCMS's 2006 International Strategy provides a start, there are insufficient mechanisms for aligning the work of British cultural institutions with the priorities of the UK government. We have set out a number of practical recommendations that could help the UK to begin to improve its position and performance. These include the review of cultural indicators by the Public Diplomacy Board as a matter of course; the establishment of financial incentives for cultural institutions to work in tune with British international priorities; the creation of international strategies by the institutions themselves; greater help and support for those seeking to work overseas; more government help to establish MoUs; and a review of the cultural diplomacy opportunities created by the London 2012 Games and the Olympiad which starts in 2008.

Culture matters – especially to the UK. It's time to start making the most of what is a special and increasingly valuable competitive edge.

3. Building relations through culture

The rise of new powers is challenging western hegemony and the structure and balance of power throughout the world. The old realities of the Cold War, with its division between rival superpowers, is now long gone, and has been replaced with a more fluid set of multilateral relationships and alliances. The UK and many other 'traditional powers' need to renegotiate their place in the world, and will do this through changing their relationships with a handful of key countries. Culture can play a critical role in this process, easing relations when they are strained, re-brokering them for changed times, and establishing fresh links in uncharted waters. However, the benefits of culture will not be fully realised unless there is a much stronger and coherent structure for coordinating the activities that contribute to cultural diplomacy. There are understandable concerns about the need to ensure that the work of cultural institutions is not instrumentalised. However, our research shows that, unless we enhance the strategic coordination of these activities, this risk is outweighed by that of missed opportunities.

The relationship between culture and politics

There is a long and intimate relationship between culture and politics. Culture can oil the cogs of the political machine in a number of ways, but is only effective when employed sensitively: it can be used as a forum for set piece political messaging, and as a safe space for unofficial political relationship-building; it can keep doors open at difficult times; and it can help to renegotiate relationships for changing times.

Getting the relationship right between politics and culture can deliver real results. Get it wrong, and relationships can be soured for a generation. Seemingly small things can have serious repercussions: India still smarts at George W Bush's failure to travel to the Taj Mahal during his 2006 visit. But a fine balance has to be struck between culture being used instrumentally for political ends, where behaviour can seem Machiavellian and both culture and politics suffer, and maintaining too much distance between the two. In international relations, the UK government adopts an arm's length relationship with the institutions of the cultural sector, who also maintain a formally arm's length, though highly cooperative, relationship with each other. The British Council, funded by the FCO rather than the DCMS, is also independent, though not immune to having its offices attacked as an agent of the British government. But distance can at times be taken too far at the expense of significant opportunities. Our national cultural institutions have an important contribution to make but are only peripherally part of the infrastructure of public diplomacy. They are too far removed from government and their overseas work does not get enough support. As a result we are missing chances to draw on their international goodwill and their deep and rich networks.

Culture can be used as a forum for unofficial political relationship-building

There is a long tradition of culture providing a safe and convivial setting for building bilateral relations or making political statements. Cultural experiences allow individuals to engage intellectually and emotionally and can provide personal connections that can outlive or override immediate political disagreements. For this reason, cultural institutions are a regular stop on the diplomatic tour, one of the few places where work and pleasure can co-exist.

In 2005, London's Royal Academy of Arts collaborated with the Palace Museum in Beijing on the exhibition *China: The Three*

Emperors, 1662–1795. The president of the Royal Academy of Arts, Sir Nicholas Grimshaw, stressed the importance of the exhibition: 'Never before has the Palace Museum made loans of such generosity; nor has it ever sent abroad so many national treasures.'[47] As the world turned its attention to the China of the computer age and the dynamism of its economy, this exhibition reminded us of China's dynamic past, a past that China is at the moment keen to stress.[48] The exhibition provided a suitable setting for the visit of the president of China, Hu Jintao, who opened it alongside the Queen in November 2005.

Six years earlier, in 1999, the Royal Ballet toured to Shanghai and Beijing to coincide with a visit by the Secretary of State for Culture, Media and Sport, Chris Smith. With Chinese leaders, including President Jiang Zemin, attending the performances, the UK ambassador to China said that he could not have dreamt of any event that would have brought the delegation in touch with so many senior members of the Chinese government. During anti-Nato protests in China, press coverage on Chinese television is estimated to have reached 600 million people.

Culture keeps doors open in difficult times

At times of political difficulty, when diplomats are not even able to sit around the negotiating table together, culture can keep doors open until relations improve. There is no better contemporary example than that of our relationship with Iran, where the election of President Mahmoud Ahmadinejad in 2005 has strained relations. Iran has a long and proud cultural history, and a cultural tradition, particularly in literature and architecture, that imbues all aspects of life. The former president, Muhammad Khatami (who responded to Samuel Huntington's Clash of Civilisations thesis with his own speech to the United Nations promoting the Dialogue among Civilisations), was once the Iranian National Librarian. In these circumstances, it is not surprising that Britain's cultural institutions are able to continue operating in Iran, thereby keeping the doors between the two countries open. As one senior former diplomat whose last posting was Iran told us: 'Our cultural institutions almost certainly have more access to the wheels of power than the UK's ambassador does at the moment.'

On the opening night of the BM's 2005 exhibition *Forgotten Empire: The world of ancient Persia*, the then British Secretary of State for Foreign Affairs, Jack Straw, was able to share a platform with the Iranian vice president, something that would have been unthinkable in any other forum. The *Financial Times* commented on the programme of discussions that were held to coincide with the exhibition: 'It was salutary to see the way that a discussion that based itself on cultural questions, indeed that sprung from the loan of a handful of ancient jewels and semi-wrecked statues, passed seamlessly on to much sharper political issues. The elision felt natural, organic.'[49]

Our cultural institutions appear to generate more trust on the part of Iran than does the BBC. Journalists from the BBC find it notoriously difficult to gain a visa to enter the country – the BBC's sole journalist in Iran is married to an Iranian – but when the directors of the Barbican and the BM wanted to record a radio programme in Iran, a BBC crew was granted special permission to travel with them. Similarly, the British Council's training for museum staff in Tehran was allowed to go ahead – and key participants were able to attend – in December 2005 when diplomatic relations were very strained.

And contact with Iran is not confined to the large institutions. In 2003 Dundee Rep performed in the country, and this year the cultural exchange organisation Visiting Arts is running workshops about business strategies in the arts at the Fadjr international theatre festival.[50]

Cultural institutions play the same role in other countries. MoMA, for instance, has continued to cooperate with Venezuelan museums despite the tension between Washington and Venezuelan president, Hugo Chavez. But the opportunities created through their work are not always taken up. For example, the National Gallery of Art in Washington, DC, has built relationships with Mexico and Guatemala over a number of years through its work on Mayan and Olmec exhibits. The gallery and its Mexican partner, the Museo Nacional de Antropología, Mexico City, agreed to hold a reciprocal show, *Obras*

Maestras, to be shown at both galleries in 1996–97. The show in Mexico was a huge success, attracting around 100,000 visitors a month, and generating a lot of public interest. The collaboration was the result of strong relations and shared interests between cultural professionals at the two institutions, and was not driven by political motives. But when the president of Mexico showed up at the exhibition's opening, an opportunity was missed because there was no US representative to meet him.

Cultural institutions are able to operate in ways that are impossible for diplomats at times of political difficulties. As many examples in this report suggest, these opportunities are often missed or under-utilised. There are numerous examples of cultural contacts enduring through periods of strained political relations, and in the past even being maintained in times of war. Examples include cultural organisations hosting a visit by Madame Ne Win of Myanmar, maintaining a scholarly research programme in North Korea,[51] and collaborating with Syria on the construction of the EU-funded website Discover Islamic Art.[52]

The FCO and British Council already collaborate on planning resource allocation to priority countries. Cultural contact is one of the best ways of ensuring that diplomatic relationships continue through difficult times. **The British government should explore the possibility of creating additional resources – financial and non-financial – to facilitate greater collaboration between the British Council, cultural institutions and organisations and their peers in priority countries.** For their part, **cultural institutions should prioritise work in these places**, and wherever possible find ways to work against market forces that would discourage their involvement. They should also **step up their work with the respective diaspora communities** in the UK through education programmes.

Culture can help to renegotiate political relationships for changing times

The rise of the BRIC countries is shifting the global balance of power and necessitating a renegotiation of relationships with these countries. For a country like the UK, the first challenge is to overcome outmoded relationships based on the assumption of western hegemony, where the West leads and dictates the terms of the debate, and the rest of the world has to fall into line. We must adapt to the rising power of emerging economies while achieving a relationship that is based on equality and respect.

Most of these emerging powers already understand the importance of cultural diplomacy in their external relations and are actively developing this aspect of their foreign policy. For India, in an era when power is a 'continuous strategic project' rather than a once and for all acquisition, culture is ever more important as a means to maintain and expand its new-found position on the world stage.[53] As the Indian prime minister put it: 'The Indian influence across much of Asia has been one of culture, language, religion, ideas and values, not of bloody conquest. We have always been respected for our traditional export, knowledge. Does that not also make India a "global superpower", though not in the traditional sense? Can this not be the power we seek in the next century?'[54]

India is engaged in a comprehensive programme of cultural diplomacy. The Indian Council for Cultural Relations is setting up offices in Washington and Paris, to complement the existing 18 offices that are mainly in places with large Indian diaspora communities. The country is currently the focus of a four-month festival of culture at the Palais des Beaux Arts in Brussels. India stole the show at the Davos World Economic Forum in January 2006 with its capture of the 'creative imperative' debate and its widely publicised campaign 'India Everywhere'. It was theme country for the Bonn Biennale, partner country for the Hanover Trade Fair and guest of honour at the Frankfurt Book Fair. In the UK, the British Museum is holding the 2006/07 Voices of Bengal Programme and the Royal Academy is staging the exhibition *Chola: Sacred Bronzes of Southern India*. India is actively using culture to expand its influence around the world.

The UK has a long and chequered history with India. Our relationship is often weighed down by heightened cultural sensitivity. As one Indian theatre director explained: 'Diplomacy doesn't work, it's too formal, too staged. To really understand each other, for creative relationships, you have to get naked in front of each other – you need trust.' One Indian museum director described how on a recent official visit by Prince Charles, staff were told by government officials to avoid even using the world 'colonial' in any conversations.

Some commentators have suggested that the UK's relationship with India has waned in recent years. According to one Indian TV producer, until fairly recently the UK commanded what he called the 'pre-eminent cultural mind space' in India: go to Kolkata with a Shakespeare performance and the audience will mouth the words along with the cast, for example. 'Doing something in the UK, whether it is a performance, an exhibition or whatever, has always brought a certain kind of recognition, a stamp of approval which opens doors in Asia and the US,' he said. However, he believes that the cumulative impact of UK cultural diplomacy could be much stronger if it refocused its energies: 'The UK stopped forcing [sic] cultural exchange and the US came to the fore in its place.'

The story of the relationship between India and the UK highlights the role that culture could play in rethinking and reinforcing cultural relationships in the service of the UK's long-term strategic interests. There is clearly an open door between the two countries, but the 'colonial hangover' can sometimes stifle diplomacy. Culture on the other hand can provide the kind of naked vulnerability that our interviewee argued is essential in building deep ties. For example, the Bhau Daji Lad in Mumbai, formerly known as the Victoria & Albert Museum, has recently been rejuvenated, with the director attributing the new success in part to the long-term expertise and support of their partners in the eight-year project, the V&A in London. He said: 'We've developed a shared culture of understanding through this project, an ability to co-create. There are so many stereotypes about relationships between the UK and India, but we've developed a new kind of understanding based on a different world view.'

For China, the ancient and imperial past is a space in which its image can be constructed to appeal to western values. China is only too aware of the scepticism with which it can be viewed by other major powers. Sustainable development and climate change are major bones of contention. Memories of Tiananmen Square linger and there are sporadic reminders in the western media that pull on the conscience of westerners seeking to cooperate with China. The vilification of the Falun Gong movement and the public and ritualistic shaming and imprisonment of prostitutes without trial in Shenzhen in late 2006 were covered with headlines like 'China witnesses a '70s flashback'.[55] Culture is a space that China wishes to keep separate from this image. Ancient and imperial culture, in particular, presents foreigners – and especially those from North America and Europe – with a framework within which they can approach China without confronting contemporary issues. This is particularly so for tourism, and visits from both North America and Europe to China (and vice versa) are on the increase.

Laying emphasis on a certain part of its cultural tradition is therefore an important feature of China's image management. In so doing, cultural diplomacy is used to appeal to pre-existing concepts of culture and value and, from the Chinese point of view, exhibitions like *China: The Three Emperors* seek to impart carefully managed meaning. In 2007/08, the BM will host *The First Emperor: China's Terracotta Army*, which will include the largest ever loan of figures from the Terracotta Army with which the First Emperor, Qin Shihuangdi, was buried. Famous the world over, these artefacts are the very heart of Chinese heritage, history and identity. Sending them to London, to occupy a space alongside the defining objects of a large number of the world's cultures, is a very significant act.

Contemporary Chinese culture is also drawing crowds. China was well represented at the 2006 Frieze Art Fair in London, and every year the streets of the world's Chinatowns are filled with people of all cultures watching dragon dancers and celebrating Chinese New Year. In 2008, there will be a series of major Chinese-themed and collaborative events when the Olympic Games are passed from China to the UK.

At a time when the UK needs to renegotiate its relations with countries like Brazil, China, India, Russia and South Africa, culture and cultural institutions can provide a crucial bridge between political negotiations and human connections, but there is currently no adequate mechanism or structure to facilitate this involvement. The FCO needs to bring cultural professionals into the heart of the decision-making process for strategies of engagement with priority countries to ensure that their insight and activities are properly taken into account. At present cultural institutions coordinate among themselves, and are members of the Public Diplomacy Stakeholders Group currently chaired by Visit Britain, which is designed to inform discussions at the Public Diplomacy Board. This needs to be revised and **cultural institutions and the DCMS should be represented on a newly formed cultural diplomacy working group run by the Public Diplomacy Group (the Secretariat of the Public Diplomacy Board)**, which would provide a formal mechanism for cultural institutions to engage with the FCO and feed into emerging thinking and policy on public diplomacy, but without skewing the focus of the whole public diplomacy strategy.

There is also a need to take specific steps to ensure that the UK diplomatic machine makes the most of the cultural opportunities that would help its work. **The FCO should ensure that all diplomats being sent to priority countries, especially the BRIC countries, are properly schooled in the culture of their new environments.** Cultural institutions could play a role in this, formally or informally, to allow the FCO to draw on the expertise of curators, performers and other cultural professionals, who might also be able to facilitate contacts on the ground. Second, **the FCO should explore the possibility of funding cultural delegations of leading cultural figures to visit the BRIC countries to build up contacts and influence and act as cultural ambassadors for the UK.**

In China, there is a special case to go further. The 2008 Beijing Olympic Games provide an opportunity for cultural diplomacy between China and the UK, who are hosting the subsequent Games. **The British Embassy and British Council in Beijing are heavily engaged in work relating to the Games and there are initial proposals for those working on the Games in the Embassy to return** to London afterwards to work on the public diplomacy strategy for London's Games. **It is vital that this arrangement extends to the cultural element, too**, and it might even be useful for one of the **British cultural institutions to second a member of staff to work with the Embassy and British Council on the Games** and come back to spread lessons and best practice to London for the start of our Olympiad in 2008. This activity should link to and build on the important work being carried out through the China–UK: Connections through Culture programme,[56] outlined in case study 2, which is being jointly funded and coordinated by the DCMS, FCO, British Council and Scottish Executive. This is one example of the type of joined-up, funded initiative that should be used as a reference point for all priority countries.

Case study 2: China–UK: Connections through Culture

China–UK: Connections through Culture (CtC) is a joint initiative between the DCMS, FCO, British Council and Scottish Executive,[57] which aims to enhance bilateral relations with China. It does this through encouraging and supporting cultural interaction. CtC provides individual cultural organisations and producers in China and the UK with the opportunity to build relationships and expertise essential for working with peers in China, and also provides support and professional development opportunities to participating organisations.

Founded on the basis of a needs analysis survey of 355 cultural organisations from the UK, mainland China and Hong Kong, CtC builds on the success of the British Council's Artist Links programme, which was run in association with ACE and provided cultural practitioners from the UK and China with the chance to study and work in the other country.[58] Participants in this scheme to whom we spoke in China greatly valued this experience, saying that it provided them with a wider cultural knowledge and exposure to a different set of professional skills that they might not otherwise have had.

CtC offers a broader platform for cultural interaction, and Artist Links provided individuals with a deeper level of experience. Both have proved valuable in nurturing cultural exchange. Developing and giving support to models that combine the two would provide the cultural basis that we will need for international relations in the future.

The relationship between culture and politics is not always benign

The reverse side of the coin of culture 'keeping doors open' is that cultural institutions sometimes work in fragile political circumstances. There are numerous examples of instances where culture has caused problems for politics, and vice versa. In December 2006, France's relations with Iran were unsettled when one of the Louvre's exhibition guides featured a map with 'the Persian Gulf' relabelled as 'the Arabian Gulf'. Iranian cultural organisations accused the museum of 'geographical revisionism', and even attempting to re-write history in the service of their substantial Arab funders.

Equally, political and judicial decisions can cause disruptions in cultural relations. The Field Museum in Chicago has been working to restore a series of cuneiform tablets on behalf of the government of Iran, and between 1948 and 2004, two-thirds of the collection was sent back, as scheduled, to Iran. However, in July 2006, a federal court upheld a decision to seize and sell off the rest of the collection held in the US, in order to raise funds to compensate Americans injured in a terrorist attack in the Middle East, based on the court's conclusion that the Islamic Republic of Iran is a state sponsor of terrorism. The case has huge implications. As Patty Gerstenblith, professor of cultural property law, DePaul University College of Law, Chicago, says: 'The question now becomes, "How do you treat cultural artefacts? Are they to be seen like any other kind of property, like land?"'[59]

It is vital that the relationship between culture and politics is carefully balanced. The British model is admired by many other countries. The UK government understands and values the inherent value of culture and its potential in international relations, but maintains an arm's length approach to avoid the political instrumentalisation of culture. This principle is underpinned institutionally by the existence of the British Council, which coordinates cultural exchange overseas to avoid the involvement of diplomatic missions. Speaking of the British Council's sister organisation, the World Service, Lord Carter said: 'If the BBC World Service were to carry a by-line stating "Working in a manner consistent with governmental medium and long-term goals" then its international credibility would be fatally undermined.'[60] However, while this approach is laudable in many respects, our research suggests that the desire to maintain the independence of national cultural institutions is too often at the expense of fruitful collaboration, and that it is possible to strengthen relations without being directive.

The UK model is in stark contrast to that of the French, which could be characterised as more 'hand-in-glove' than 'arm's length'. The former head of the French Institute in London, the cultural arm of the Ministry of Foreign Affairs, summed it up: 'la culture, c'est la politique' (culture is politics). With official cultural diplomacy activities jointly funded by the Ministry for Culture and Communication and the Ministry for Foreign Affairs, there are 154 Services for Cooperation and Cultural Activities in embassies and 436 overseas cultural institutes, of which 283 are the language-focused Alliances Françaises. In 2006, France created a new institution 'Cultures France' (modelled in many ways on the British Council) with the aim of grouping disparate diplomatic activities under one identity.

The degree to which France integrates the structures of diplomacy with those of culture would be a step too far for the UK, whose cultural institutions guard their independence fiercely, strongly supported by their government. But France highlights the benefits that can be gained when a government works more collaboratively and strategically with culture and understands the wealth of benefits it can generate. **We cannot expect these partnerships to happen by** chance, and they must be underpinned by strong governance arrangements to ensure that the correct balance is always maintained between cultural integrity and political imperatives. As suggested above, the creation of a cultural diplomacy group within the public diplomacy structure at the FCO would provide an important forum for cultural institutions to have formal involvement in strategy development and would also act as a regular point of linkage between them and the FCO.

The implications for the British Council relate to the focus and emphasis of their work, rather than a wholesale overhaul of their mission. The UK's independent model is admired the world over, and this value should remain at the heart of British approaches to cultural diplomacy. The British Council should be measured more on its ability to broker and match-make, and on the richness and depth of its networks, than on its ability to generate column inches or the number of people attending its own events. This report has shown that the British cultural 'product' is good – we have world-class artists and performers and our institutions are respected the world over. They should be allowed to speak for themselves, with the British Council providing platforms and support behind the scenes, including the one-stop-shop unit recommended in chapter 2, which lies beyond their current remit.

One of the most important conclusions in this chapter is that the UK needs to let go of its hang-ups about the relationship between politics and culture. Given our starting position, there are few immediate risks of the relationship becoming too close, although this should be closely and regularly monitored. **The really big risks come from not acting, from missed opportunities, and from our competitors stealing the strategic edge over us.** Culture is so often described as a 'soft' tool, but our analysis argues that there is nothing fluffy or nebulous about culture and its contribution to public diplomacy. With a strategic overview, a more coordinated approach, targeted funding and enhanced support, the UK could use its rich resources to meet the competition, but only if it acts now, and only if it acts decisively and takes some risks.

4. Next generation cultural diplomacy

This report has shown how and why culture should play a role in public diplomacy as a distinct activity, broadly defined as cultural diplomacy. It has set out a practical agenda for integrating the work of cultural institutions into the existing structures and working practices of public diplomacy, primarily driven through the FCO and the British Council. The world does not stand still, though, and in the future, the public diplomacy dividend will increasingly go to countries that respond to the challenges and opportunities posed by the latest phase of globalisation.

New York Times columnist Thomas Friedman, in his book *The World is Flat*, calls this Globalisation 3.0.[61] The rise of new technologies, the new possibilities offered by the internet, the growth of global communication and the proliferation of cheap international travel are providing individual citizens with the tools to influence politics from the comfort – and anonymity – of their own homes. Friedman argues that the countries that will be the leaders of tomorrow are those that have the infrastructure to connect with these new technological platforms, equip their citizens with the tools and capacity to cope, and have structures of governance in place to manage the potential negative side effects.

We must not underestimate the enormity of the cumulative impact of the changes described; they challenge the basis of current public diplomacy policy and practices, and require wholesale systemic change and adaptation. This chapter sets out a number of specific recommendations that could help the government, British Council and UK cultural institutions to respond to these changes, but ultimately a piecemeal approach will not suffice. We need to change institutional mindsets, embrace new partnership models of working, and ensure that new technologies drive the work of these institutions, rather than be treated as added extras to their current activities. Tinkering around the edges will not be enough, and it will require the investment of energy and time, as well as money.

The rise of new technologies and the internet

The forces of globalisation used to be the preserve of countries and corporations, but now, globalisation has reached the level of the individual. Friedman's concept of Globalisation 3.0 describes a new era in the globalisation process that began at the start of the new millennium. While the first period was characterised by the globalisation of *countries*, and the second by that of *companies*, the defining characteristic of this new era is the ability of *individuals* to reap the benefits of globalisation and connect with other people on a truly global level. Thanks to computers, email, fibre-optic networks, teleconferencing and dynamic new software it is possible for individuals to collaborate and compete in real time with more people from more corners of the planet on more kinds of work and on a more equal footing than ever before.

Friedman argues:

> *This platform now operates without regard to geography, distance, time, and, in the near future, even language. . . . Wealth and power will increasingly accrue to those countries, companies, individuals, universities, and groups who get three basic things right: the infrastructure to connect with this flat-world platform, the education to get more of their people innovating on, working off, and tapping into this platform, and, finally, the governance to get the best out of this platform and cushion its worst side effects.*[62]

While the two previous periods of globalisation were western-led, the new era will see the rise of non-western countries, especially places like China and India, but also parts of the developing world where mobile phone technology is increasing internet connectivity. These possibilities are particularly interesting for a country like China, where there have been few channels for individual expression. As case study 3 shows, ordinary Chinese people are beginning to use the internet to communicate, express themselves and organise in ways that were previously impossible. While connectivity is currently limited to urban areas in countries such as China and India, there is no room for complacency about our own capacities. As Friedman's quote above reminds us, governments, institutions and individuals must respond quickly to the challenges and opportunities of the new phase of globalisation. Soon, the relative advantage of the West – especially English-speaking countries – could be lost due to the scale of the challenge from the emerging powers.

> ### Case study 3: Underground filmmaking in Beijing
> In Beijing we met an underground filmmaker, who by day works for the state-run channel, CCTV, and by night makes his own 'unofficial', privately funded movies for underground circulation. Just a few years ago, his night-time work would have been strictly a small-scale hobby, accessible to only a narrow range of people. But with the help of the internet, the falling price of digital equipment and a persistent ignorance on the part of the Chinese government of the real potential of the internet as a medium for such work, he is able to reach a much bigger audience.
>
> He also runs a website which gives help and advice to aspiring filmmakers. On the site they can get tips on perfecting a range of filmmaking techniques, the latest news about equipment, and other information that will help them to perfect their art form. Their filmmaking tends to focus on the lives of ordinary people. In a country like China, whose government takes a very keen interest in the way that China is portrayed to the outside world, this is

potentially destabilising. As we were leaving the studio, two of the filmmaker's colleagues were editing a film which depicted life in a small town about an hour to the north of Beijing. As he told us: 'The government is afraid that our films might reveal a dark aspect of Chinese society, such as poverty or corruption, which might give rise to public riots.' Another Chinese independent filmmaker made a similar point: 'The internet is God's gift to the Chinese people.'

The British Council already invests heavily in IT-based services to support and extend the reach of its projects, for example its permanent collection of twentieth- and twenty-first-century art is online; *Crossing Borders* provides IT-based mentoring for young African writers; and video-conferencing facilities are available in many BC offices, allowing them to run Café Scientifique-type events. Technology is changing fast, though, in particular the introduction of social software which is causing a groundshift in culture and cultural engagement. **The British Council should therefore invest in training programmes for all staff in the latest technological trends**, such as wikis, social software and podcasts, to ensure that these tools are always driving their work rather than treated as add-ons to more traditional tools, such as events, publications and exchanges.

The rise of social software and social networking tools means that people are connecting, organising and collaborating in new ways. **We recommend that the British Council develops its own social software platforms within the countries in which it operates to help it coordinate the growing numbers of cultural players on the ground.** This would allow any cultural institution visiting the country or city to log on to the site to post details about their activities without the need for mediation by British Council staff. Through web facilities such as this, the British Council would instantly position itself at the centre of cultural life in the countries in which it operates and provide an additional useful service for their partners and those interested in engaging with UK culture.

Implications for cultural institutions

The internet has become a basic and important tool for all the UK's major cultural institutions; no major concert hall, theatre, gallery or any other institution could survive without a website, an online booking service and an email update. Many are developing their websites to act as virtual versions of their physical work. From photographing and describing paintings and objects on searchable databases, to digitising content, they are investing more time and money in creating vast stores of online content. Sometimes this is done in innovative ways, such as the British Library's 'Turning the Page' project where viewers can see images of fragile and valuable books and turn their pages by touching a screen, as well as finding out related information. Sometimes it takes a simpler form, such as straightforward online catalogues. Funding for these initiatives has come from a variety of sources, which transcend borders and boundaries. Microsoft is funding the British Library's digitisation of nineteenth-century novels, and the digitisation work of Kew's African Plants Initiative is funded entirely by US foundations. In 2006, the British Museum gave a Chinese professor a residency, during which he helped to catalogue and digitise the BM's collections of Chinese paintings as part of a wider programme of skills sharing in both directions.

At a time when culture has assumed a new relevance to international relations, and given the fact that access is such an important driver for cultural institutions, it is vital that these developments continue at a brisk pace. It would also be desirable for them, wherever possible, to reflect the UK's international priorities. Towards these ends, **the government should explore options for supporting the development of the online aspect of the work of cultural institutions**. This might not necessarily mean more funding, but the sharing of expertise and best practice. **Where funding is allocated, preference should be given to initiatives that focus on current priorities,** such as projects that would enhance relations with the Middle East or with diasporas, or that would contribute towards the reduction in climate change.

On a more fundamental level, the internet is also changing the nature of culture and the nature of the culture that we consume, and far from replacing actual experience, virtual engagement has proved a stimulus to physical participation. Visitors to London's Science Museum can engage with its exhibit *Who am I?* not just within the walls of its South Kensington home, but also from wherever they can access a computer. Theatres, like the National Theatre, provide podcasts that offer expert commentary and behind-the-scenes glimpses.[63]

People now expect not just to be able to access culture virtually, but also want the opportunity to add their own opinion. This represents more than personalisation of choice: it means that individuals can shape and share the meaning of culture. In New York, prior to their visit, museum-goers to the Museum of Modern Art can not only download podcasts that provide information about the works in the collection, but also contribute their own thoughts by uploading their own comment pieces. In the UK, museums like the V&A and Tate have offered similar opportunities. The *Guardian* has opened curation to the public through the project 'Your Gallery'. Its success 'proves once again that people do not want to abandon the physical work of art, only to find new ways to communicate it'.[64] On the website of Cleveland Museum in the US, curators have opened the categories by which their collections can be searched to public opinion. Now, paintings can be searched for by both orthodox terms, like 'Impressionist' and 'Woman', but also terms that users can determine according to their own interests, building collections which they can then share with other users. **Cultural institutions should continue to develop these kinds of online services for their visitors.**

Technology is also being used to engage new audiences through projects such as Plant Cultures.[65] Taking the communities of South Asia (India, Pakistan and Bangladesh), the site uses oral history, fine arts and demonstrations of arts and crafts to bring to life the ways in which plants are used in different communities. The lead project partner is the Royal Botanic Gardens, Kew, which is working alongside regional partners: the Museum of London, Leicester City Museums and National Museums Liverpool. All these organisations work with local community groups to create web-based content that reflects the diverse ways in which South Asian families use plants in their everyday lives. As the next section on diaspora communities will show, these kinds of initiatives are important for bridging between communities, and providing important links between 'home' and 'abroad'.

Immigration and diaspora communities

Given the high level of immigration to the UK over the past 30 years, diaspora communities have become an important and constant feature of life in Britain; there are citizens of almost every country living and working in the UK. The relationships between these communities and their countries of origin have strengthened over this period as a result of the growth of affordable international travel and instant global communication. Today, something said in Leicester will reach Bangladesh quicker than you could fly there, and vice versa. As one curator from the BM observed, 'What happens in Mumbai feeds back, electronically and physically, immediately into UK communities.' 'Home and abroad' has ceased to be a meaningful distinction.

While the importance of these links has been acknowledged rhetorically, it is often difficult to embody them in practical policy suggestions or changed ways of working. This is partly because the FCO's mandate is broadly speaking *outside* the UK, and there are always dilemmas for civil servants about when to extend overseas work at home without stepping on the toes of other *domestic* government departments. In recent years, the FCO has increased the number of staff responsible for liaising with diaspora communities in the UK, which is a welcome development. But there is still a tendency for this work to be regarded as 'outreach' or communication, rather than two-way engagement. One civil servant from the FCO commented: 'There are very real misperceptions of our policy that we need to correct. That has to be our first priority.'

There is also nervousness about getting input on policy from minority or diaspora communities for fear that this is seen as preferential treatment or access. A recent Demos report[66] argued for the need to open up the foreign policy-making process to all communities, but especially those who feel alienated by the government's current foreign policy in certain parts of the world, notably the Middle East and wider Islamic world. **We echo this proposal, and suggest that the FCO and DCMS should work in partnership with the Department for Communities and Local Government (DCLG) to create a comprehensive strategy for engagement with minority and diaspora communities through culture.** As Friedman's Globalisation 3.0 takes hold, it is vital that the UK realises the full potential offered by its rich network of diaspora communities, which could play key roles as the UK's 'everyday ambassadors'.

Cultural institutions have understood the potential of working with communities in the UK, to connect them better to their work and to bring additional insight to their exhibitions and work schemes. Case study 4 from the V&A provides an excellent example of the ways in which such projects can build strong and trusted relationships and reinforce the importance of these diasporas to UK culture and identity. Similarly, the BM's 2006 Voices of Bengal programme involved South Asian communities in the UK in a substantive and an advisory capacity, and the V&A and the British Library regularly hold special events for specific communities and involve them in the production of their work. Some of this activity generates coverage overseas as well as in the UK, which can help to highlight the UK's openness to other cultures and people. For example, the BM's exhibition *Forgotten Empire* was covered widely in the Iranian press.

Case study 4: V&A's Shamiana project

In the V&A's Shamiana project, South Asian women of all ages had the opportunity to work together to create original textile panels in styles inspired by the collections of the V&A and other museums. Some of this work was strongly rooted in traditional South Asian

---

textile traditions and skills, while other pieces revealed the interaction of contemporary British and Asian cultures and art forms. The project sparked the formation of women's groups to create panels throughout Britain, which then extended to other countries, including Ireland, the Middle East, South Africa and the US.

The project's exhibition at the V&A in 1997 brought nearly 100 of these works together, and then toured to other countries. Some of the panels created by community groups were acquired on merit by the Asian Department for the permanent collections, and a book was published to document the project.[67]

The project demonstrates how the work of cultural institutions can build links with diaspora communities, facilitate contact between these communities and those overseas, and convey an important message about the centrality of them and their culture to the UK, thus reaffirming their identity.

This work is essential for the UK if it is to tap into diaspora communities as a powerful asset. But while collaborations such as those shown in case study 4 can be hugely rewarding and offer all sorts of benefits beyond the cultural, such as community relations, goodwill and effective youth engagement, cultural institutions often struggle through a lack of resources. Other countries are wise to the opportunities afforded by their diaspora communities. For example, India even has a government ministry dedicated to its international diaspora – the Ministry of Overseas Indian Affairs.

As acknowledged above, one of the stumbling blocks is the continuing – but false – division between home and abroad. In funding terms, this can tend to separate work that delivers benefit in the UK from that overseas, which means that work streams tend to become siloed. Although there are examples of cultural institutions working together in this area, there are currently few incentives, besides those offered by the market. **In order to begin to break down these barriers we suggest that, as part of the DCMS's new**

International Strategy, it builds the capacity to act as a liaision point between cultural institutions and diaspora communities in the UK, with the priority placed on those communities that are important in foreign policy terms. In fulfilling this function, the DCMS would need to liaise closely with the FCO and ensure that any activities in the UK are properly linked to and referenced against work carried out by diplomatic missions and British Council offices overseas.

As well as facilitating relationships and activities for individual institutions and small groups working together, **there is also scope for the DCMS to coordinate more public and participatory events that would have the added benefit of highlighting the contribution of diaspora communities to the British public as a whole.** One model that might be useful in this regard is that of France's Saisons Culturels, the organisation and purpose of which are explained in case study 5.

Case study 5: Saisons Culturels

France's Saisons Culturels are explicitly political, and highly coordinated. One country is invited each year by the Ministry of Foreign Affairs and the Ministry of Culture and Communication to be the focus of a series of exhibitions and events (dance, theatre, cinema, music, art) focusing on its culture. The intention is to create long-lasting relationships.

The size of the programmes and events varies depending on the country – China (2000/01), for example, was a major undertaking, and included 'France in China' exhibitions in China, as well as 'China in France' exhibitions in France. Twenty companies donated 500,000 euros each, supported by a number of other endowments. Although government support was extensive, only 4–5 million euros of public money was involved. It is difficult to judge the precise impact of these cumulative activities, but indicators that it was effective include a tripling of Chinese visitors to the Louvre in the last year. The 'saison' model is not without controversy, with institutions like the Pompidou Centre particularly vociferous about

---

their fears of being instrumentalised by government. The 'saison' model is not confined to France – Belgium, Poland and Russia all have similar programmes.

While it would be impossible to import this model wholesale – France and the UK have very different approaches to cultural diplomacy – **there is a case for adapting the Saison Culturel model, appointing 'creative directors' to animate, oversee and coordinate relationships with strategically important countries and their diasporas in the UK, perhaps involving the type of public festivals that have become popular in recent years.** A nationally coordinated 'saisons' model could then be adapted and rolled out at the local level by local authorities and city governments.

Building cultural literacy

Next generation public diplomacy will be conducted in a world where individual citizens have more power and opportunity to dictate or influence the terms of debate than ever before. Public diplomacy expert Thomas Risse has stressed the growing importance of understanding and operating at this local or personal level: 'To achieve true understanding of nations and peoples, it is imperative that the two parties engage in both persuading and being open to be persuaded by the other. Such engagement represents the mode of dialogic communication, and can probably be most effectively pursued and accomplished at the local level.'[68] **Where the rise of public diplomacy could be described as the shift from few-to-few communication (traditional diplomacy) to few-to-many, this era will be characterised by the growth of many-to-many interactions** between individual citizens and groups of citizens, where formal intervention or mediation will be much more difficult. It is vital that the UK's institutions of public and cultural diplomacy respond to this new context quickly and effectively.

Today, individuals and groups are able to shift public opinion and mobilise for change. There are many recent examples. The 2006 row over the publication in a Danish newspaper of cartoons depicting the Prophet Muhammad escalated on internet chatrooms and blogs and led to the sale of Danish goods plummeting across the Middle East, accompanied by rioting and attacks on some Nordic embassies in Syria and Lebanon. Similarly, British Chancellor Gordon Brown found himself embroiled in a diplomatic incident during his visit to India early in 2007, caused by the treatment of one of the country's most renowned Bollywood actresses by a British reality TV star in the UK Celebrity Big Brother house. On a more positive note, 'Brand UK' looks set to receive a handsome dividend when footballer David Beckham transfers to play in the US. As the academic and former US Information Agency (USIA) staffer Richard Arndt put it: 'Cultural relations grow naturally and organically, without government intervention – the transactions of trade and tourism, student flows, communications, book circulation, migration, media access, inter-marriage – [there are] millions of daily cross-cultural encounters.'[69]

We are no longer represented just by our leaders. Knowingly or not, we are all representatives of our countries and we have the tools to make an impact. We are all diplomats now. **It is therefore critical that we ensure that our British citizens – especially young people – have the skills and capacity to cope with this new era of global cultural connection.** While Samuel Huntington's 'Clash of Civilisations' theory is contested, the new century has certainly been marked by a *collision* of civilisations and it is vital that the UK equips itself and its citizens to guide themselves through this new terrain.

The UK must ensure that its citizens are culturally literate. This does not just mean teaching our children about the cultures, histories and societies of other parts of the world, although this is clearly important. The pace of cultural interaction and change means that individuals will need the capacity to make real-time choices and conclusions necessary for navigating diversity, recognising signals and getting on with other cultures against an ever-changing backdrop. Cultural literacy is about creating the capacity to interpret, rather than simply building up stores of knowledge. It is also underpinned by a belief that being able to relate to other cultures starts from an understanding of your own, as recognised in recent recommendations about the teaching of citizenship.[70]

One of the British Council's objectives relates to increasing the international outlook and understanding of young people in the UK, and the kind of mutual understanding and appreciation embodied in the idea of cultural literacy is at the heart of their work. There is scope to build on this through the work of cultural institutions, both independently of, and in partnership with, the British Council.

Most cultural institutions already have education and learning programmes where they use their exhibitions, performances and programmes as a way of helping young people and other generations to learn about the rest of the world and themselves. However, the national need – let alone the international potential – dwarfs their current capacity. **We make recommendations elsewhere about the need to increase the capacity for cultural institutions to increase their learning work, especially with diaspora communities, but this needs to be extended on a larger national scale, too, perhaps coordinated through the DCMS and DfES.**

In New York we came across an interesting programme that could act as a central component for a strategy for cultural literacy carried out in partnership with cultural institutions, set out in case study 6. 'The Art of Observation' programme at the Frick Collection uses art substantively to improve observational skills, and heighten people's awareness of the fact that we all see things differently based on our experiences and prejudices. As Amy Herman, the programme's creator, told us, it is important that people are given the opportunity to discuss their prejudices in a safe way and reflect on the substantive impacts this has on themselves and others. She said: 'One of the medical students who did the programme was asked to describe a painting of an obese black woman. He went round the houses, outlining everything in the picture apart from the two things that could have been critical to her medical diagnosis in a hospital – her weight and skin colour. It really took him aback when we discussed this and made him question the way in which he conducts his patient diagnoses. It was critical that he had the space to explore these issues and art provides a safe context in which this can happen.'

The US Embassy in Spain has supported a presentation of the programme in Madrid, and so impressed were the officials in attendance that they have asked for similar training to be given to foreign service officers. **The government should explore the possibility of running a similar scheme through cultural institutions in the UK.**

Case study 6: The Art of Observation at the Frick Collection

The private Frick Collection runs a programme called 'The Art of Observation', which works with a range of professionals – from FBI and CIA agents to police officers and medical students – using art to improve their observational skills. The day begins with a presentation outlining some of the basic principles of effective observation, which gives the group a chance to discuss the factors that might influence their ability to see a situation, crime scene or accident scene objectively, picking up as many cues as possible. They then carry out observational sessions in groups, each working on a different painting (it could work equally well with a range of cultural mediums, such as museum artefacts or dance performances). Each person describes what they see in the 'scene' (painting): what is happening, who the people in the painting are, how they found themselves in that position, and so on. They then come back together to discuss what they have 'seen'.

As well as developing the cultural literacy of key professionals and leaders, such as those involved in the programme at the Frick, it is also vital that the UK's cultural literacy initiatives incorporate the wider range of 'opinion formers' created by this latest phase of globalisation. The British Council has worked hard in recent years to extend its reach. We came across an interesting example of this in India. Mocha, a chain of trendy coffee shops in Mumbai, is a regular haunt for students at top Indian universities like the Indian Institute of Technology (IIT) Bombay. The British Council put on a series of events in Mocha featuring top Indian and British DJs and comedians with the aim of taking the message of British creativity to a previously inaccessible audience. By taking these discussions out to the places these kinds of people frequent, it was hoped that the young people who attended would start to associate the UK with creativity and cutting-edge music.

The British Council's renewed focus on 18–35-year-olds also plays well into this agenda. Culture, particularly music and film, is a great way of reaching this group. For example, in Ethiopia, where 44 per cent of the population is under the age of 15, and only 3 per cent over the age of 65,[71] it is vital to engage the upcoming generation, which does not form part of the current structures of power. In Addis Ababa, the British Council is working both with the established structures of government-backed culture, such as the National Archive and Library of Ethiopia and the National Theatre, *and* with young people through literature, music and film. **Activities like the Mumbai DJ project should be rolled out by other British Council offices around the world; it should also ensure that it has the right structures in place to share latest thinking about best practice about accessing the hard to reach younger generation.**

Coming to terms with a pick and mix approach to national image

One of the natural consequences of the rise of many-to-many public diplomacy is the challenge of maintaining a relatively coherent national 'story' or image. As the level of exchange increases, it will become harder to be consistent in terms of message. Our understanding of our national image will therefore require a more pragmatic, pick and mix approach.

We are already beginning to see this dilemma play out. On the one hand, the UK has fought hard to shake off outmoded images of Olde Englishness as economic and social changes have taken hold. On the other, there is value to be gained from some of these stereotypes. Many Chinese families are keen to send their children to be educated in the UK because of their assumptions about standards and a reverence for the country's traditions and past. Public schools and universities have been quick to realise the potential: Dulwich College opened a branch in China in Shanghai, which was inaugurated by Tony Blair in July 2003, and Harrow soon followed suit. A further branch of Dulwich College will open in Suzhou in 2007 and a recent Beijing imitation has styled itself 'Eton'.[72]

Multiple national identities – the thatched cottage sitting alongside Tate Modern – should not be a cause for alarm: 'If we are living in the shadow of an older identity, it is not because this identity is somehow more authentic than any other. It is rather because the original invention of Britishness was so successful . . . that it has proven extraordinarily difficult to update it.'[73] Ensuring that the full range of cultural actors are involved in delivering the UK's public and cultural diplomacy is one way of ensuring that the richness of the UK's national character is fully on display.

This chapter has argued that public diplomacy is undergoing a period of intense change as new technologies, global communications and the rise of immigration and travel take hold. The UK public diplomacy machine must respond to this wholesale, rather than adopt small-scale and piecemeal changes. We are witnessing the emergence of a next generation of public diplomacy and the scale of our response must be proportionate to the scale of change. We make a number of recommendations relating to the need to embrace new technologies, realise the potential offered by diaspora communities, and embark on a new national strategy of cultural literacy to ensure British citizens are equipped for the challenge of increased global cultural exchange. One of the key messages is that old distinctions between 'home' and 'abroad' are outmoded and government and institutional structures and working arrangements need to reflect this. One of the key challenges will be for the DCMS in realising its ambition to be the engine house for a new international cultural policy. If it can effectively broker relations between cultural activities and communities in the UK, the activities of cultural institutions overseas and the work of the FCO and our diplomatic missions overseas, this will represent important progress in eradicating the dangers of silo working.

5. Conclusions and recommendations

This report has argued that culture is a key component of UK public diplomacy. The UK has historical advantages: its collections and performing companies are world class, we have highly skilled and respected cultural professionals, we are home to world-class artists, our culture and heritage act as magnets for tourism and business, our creative industries are strong and we have a wealth of relationships with traditional and emerging powers alike, not least through the British Council's presence around the globe. And from 2008 onwards the eyes of the world will be focused on London as it begins its Olympiad ahead of the 2012 Olympic Games.

While the UK currently has a cultural competitive advantage, we must not rest on our laurels. We are investing less than the US and our European neighbours in our cultural institutions, there are few formal mechanisms for engaging these organisations and other cultural leaders in the policy-making process, and while there are many examples of good practice, our work also highlights missed opportunities. Some of our competitors, on the other hand, are playing a much more strategic game. Particularly important to note is the emphasis that emerging powers like China and India are placing on the role of culture in international relations. If the twenty-first century really is going to belong to these countries, then we need to make sure that we are placing sufficient emphasis on culture, too.

An ambitious programme of change is needed, and this report has recommendations for the UK government, British Council and the main cultural institutions. These are divided into five broad areas: building effective governance systems, developing political leadership, using the Olympics as a focus for partnership working, cultural literacy, and responding to the challenges and opportunities posed by new technologies.

Building effective governance systems

We will not realise the potential of culture in international relations by chance. If we are serious about making the most of the UK's cultural competitive argument, we need a sound system of governance to oversee this work and create more partnership working arrangements between the government, British Council and the cultural institutions. This report recommends that:

O   cultural institutions and the DCMS should be represented
     on a newly formed Cultural Diplomacy working group,
     run by the Public Diplomacy Group at the FCO
O   the Cultural Diplomacy working group would have a
     number of responsibilities, but specifically it would:
     O   agree priorities for UK cultural diplomacy
     O   regularly review relevant indicators to assess the state
          of the UK's cultural competitive position
     O   assess where official government intervention or
          action might be helpful, such as government-to-
          government MoUs.

The UK must find ways to incentivise our cultural institutions to conduct work that contributes towards the UK's international priorities. There are a number of ways it could do this:

O   Those cultural institutions that have not already done so
     should create international strategies, whose partial
     function would be to show where their international work
     matches the UK's international priorities. Their creation

and sharing of the plans – through the Cultural Diplomacy working group – would also help to develop a better understanding within government of what the cultural sector is doing, and what it has to offer.

○ The government should create a one-stop-shop assistance unit for British cultural institutions wishing to work outside the UK. Run by the British Council, this would provide information, assistance, partnering and so forth to help lower the barriers to entry.

○ A modest fund should be created to support training and development in the UK of overseas cultural professionals.

○ There should also be a small fund to support first-time collaboration by UK cultural institutions in the priority countries and opportunities to collaborate that their current funding structures may restrict.

○ The British Council should explore opportunities to promote more long-term collaboration between UK cultural institutions and priority countries.

○ The government should trial a new visa system that would seek to make cultural exchange easier.

○ The FCO should explore the possibility of funding cultural delegations of leading cultural figures to the BRIC countries to build up contacts and influence and to act as cultural ambassadors for the UK.

○ DCMS should consider investing in creative directors to nurture cultural relationships with priority countries.

Developing political leadership

Structure alone will not be enough: to build momentum, the UK needs clear political leadership highlighting the value of culture in international relations. For example:

○ Ministers and their government departments must look for more opportunities to engage leading cultural professionals in the policy-making process through their involvement in policy teams and commissions.

O Government should ensure that the UK's cultural standing is maintained by continuing to invest in our asset base across a wide field (from collections, to the capacity to keep producing world-class performers) and by continuing to invest in the means through which those assets are best exploited and cared for (from buildings to technology and beyond).

O Government should invest in a range of resources appropriate to context. This report has highlighted that different approaches are needed in different places. Different government departments, in partnership with cultural institutions, need to respond appropriately. For example, the primary need in Africa is for money and capacity-building, while the primary need in China is for political, diplomatic and on-the-ground coordination. This means different partnerships should come together, underpinned by different types of resources.

Using the Olympics as a focus for partnership working

Inevitably, implementing the kind of change we are proposing will involve a lot of work. The forthcoming Olympiad offers a sustained period in the run-up to 2012 for focusing the national mind around the importance of culture to our place in the world. The UK must seize this opportunity and in the process assert our international standing. We must:

O ensure that the FCO's public diplomacy strategy is joined up with DCMS and LOCOG plans for the Cultural Olympiad. By doing this, cultural diplomacy can be made a central theme in the 2012 public diplomacy strategy, both at home and abroad

O create a team of cultural ambassadors for the Olympic Games

○ utilise the opportunity posed by the 2008 Games to
improve UK–China relations. In order to do this, one or
more cultural institutions could second staff to work
alongside embassy officials in Beijing on the UK's public
diplomacy strategy for the Games. These people could
then return to London following the Games to feed in
ideas and thinking for 2012.

Cultural literacy

The growth of new technologies, global communications, travel,
migration and new democratic expectations of citizens means that we
are all diplomats now. This is especially true for a country like the
UK, which has so many external links. This can be a challenge as well
as an opportunity, and we need to ensure that we are well equipped to
deal with this new reality. We recommend that:

○ the government should conduct a root and branch review
of the way in which we school our young people to ensure
they have the skills and capacity to cope with this new era
of global cultural connection
○ the British Council continues to develop projects that
reach 18–35-year-olds in the UK and abroad, especially
those who are hard to reach
○ the government and cultural institutions, via the Cultural
Diplomacy working group, should explore the possibility
of replicating the Art of Observation initiative, and
develop other cultural literacy initiatives
○ the FCO and DCMS should work in partnership with
the DCLG to create a comprehensive strategy for
engagement with minority and diaspora communities
through culture
○ the DCMS should explore the possibility of coordinating
more public and participatory events to highlight the
contribution of diaspora and minority communities to
the UK

○ the FCO should ensure that all diplomats being sent to priority countries, especially the BRIC countries, are properly schooled in the culture of their new environments; this should be done on a programmatic rather than an ad hoc basis.

Responding to the challenges and opportunities posed by new technologies

For many years, there has been a growing recognition of the impact of new technologies, but our institutions have been slow to get to grips with them. Too often, technologies are tacked on to old working practices, rather than being the basis for new ones. If the UK is to stay ahead of the pack on cultural diplomacy, this must be addressed as a matter of urgent priority. There are number of practical steps we could take:

○ The FCO and British Council must invest in training programmes for all staff in the latest technological trends and their application to policy-making.
○ The government should explore options for supporting the development of the online aspect of the work of cultural institutions. Where funding is allocated, preference should be given to initiatives that focus on priority countries.
○ British Council offices should run their websites using social software that allows partners and other cultural organisations to input information about their work in-country. This will help to make the British Council the point of reference, coordination and match-making in each country it works in.
○ In their emerging online strategy, the Olympic organising bodies should ensure that there is significant cultural content, exchange and user participation, reflecting the leadership of the UK in this field.

Appendix: Snapshots of cultural diplomacy

China, Ethiopia, France, India, Norway and the US

China

Like France, culture and politics are closely linked. The Chinese government is conscious of the appeal that ancient and imperial culture has. It is also aware of the appeal of modern, urban and youthful Chinese culture. At the same time, however, it is wary of many of the attitudes and technologies that lie behind this. Websites, blogs and other new platforms enable communication and the expression of opinion that are increasingly difficult to control and monitor and the government has recently begun to crack down on the use of the internet in China.

Culture is a particularly useful tool for China in developing its international relations as it provides an alternative focus for partnerships from the more contentious issues, such as human rights, democracy and the environment. The dynamism of its contemporary culture also fits neatly with the booming interest in China's economy and rise overseas. In this narrative, the ancient past is a useful reminder that China is not so much 'rising', as reasserting its status. The naming of Chinese overseas cultural institutes 'Confucius Institutes' at once reinforces the ancient roots of Chinese culture, the appeal of that culture overseas and the 'peaceful' nature of China's resurgence, an image that the country's leaders are keen to assert.

Policy home base

Cultural diplomacy is not so much a discrete policy owned by any given department, as bound up within foreign policy, the presentation of domestic policy overseas, and internal control. Major institutions like the Palace Museum are state-run, and their directors are party members and state officials. The Palace Museum director has the status of a vice minister of culture, as does the director of the National Museum of China. The Palace Museum describes itself as 'the cultural business card of China'.

Funding

It is difficult to get an accurate picture of funds devoted to 'cultural diplomacy', although general cultural funding provides a clue. Where national museums receive about 80 per cent of their funding from the state, regional museums get about 40–50 per cent; they have to earn the rest. Similarly, the Peking Opera, a national symbol, gets 80 per cent of its funding from the state.

Infrastructure

Chinese embassies overseas are accompanied by a strong network of cultural attachés, and are increasingly supported by the work of the newly created Confucius Institutes.

New developments

Conceived in 2004, 100 Confucius Institutes are planned around the world in the next five years – they represent a definite use of culture to build knowledge and familiarity with China overseas and are broadly speaking comparable with the French Alliance Française. The National Office for Teaching Chinese as a Foreign Language (NOCFL), the Hanban, is also selecting, training and providing living expenses for hundreds of Chinese volunteers to teach Mandarin in 23 different countries: in 2005, there were 10,000 volunteers waiting for placements.

Ethiopia

Ethiopia has an immensely rich and ancient culture. It is the site of the discoveries of the earliest human remains, and has many distinctive cultures, from the Christian north, to the Muslim west to the tribal south. The country was never colonised (a very brief period of Italian occupation of parts of the country does not qualify), but has suffered years of instability and conflict, and parts of the country have experienced severe drought and famine. Ethiopia struggles to preserve and maintain its heritage – the National Museum has no fully trained conservator for example – although there are many areas of progress, such as new building at the National Museum and the Ethiopia Flora Project. UK institutions are involved in assisting this development and in capacity-building, but so are the Americans, French, Germans, Italians, Japanese and Swedes. In 2007 there is a unique opportunity for cultural cooperation: it is the Ethiopian millennium. The British Council is an important organisation in Addis Ababa. Historically its library, opened soon after the end of the Second World War, has been a vital resource for generations of Ethiopians. With a very young, and large, population, some of the world's most significant cultural and scientific sites and artefacts, poor infrastructure and lack of resources, Ethiopia presents particular challenges and opportunities in terms of cultural development and relations.

France

Culture and politics are perceived as closely linked, although funding for culture in France is becoming more distributed (eg the Louvre has increased fundraising staff from five to 25 in the past five years). This still leaves high levels of central funding and coordination of cultural institutions, which provide strategic opportunities for collaborative cultural 'seasons'. These are highly successful, but not uncontroversial, with some cultural institutions voicing concerns about instrumentalisation by political actors. The prospective opening of a Louvre museum in Abu Dhabi is one such area of contention. Supporting *francophonie* is still a central strand of cultural diplomacy policy, although it is often seen by cultural institutions as a kind of French Commonwealth – a global region of interest within which funding for cultural activities is particularly easy to access.

Policy home base

Cultural diplomacy policy is jointly owned by the Ministry of Foreign Affairs and the Ministry of Culture and Communication (Directorate of International Affairs).

Funding

It is difficult to get an accurate picture of funds devoted to 'cultural diplomacy', although the Directorate for International Cooperation and Development within the Ministry of Foreign Affairs had a budget of 2.2 billion euros in 2005. Four-fifths of this is designated as public aid for development. A considerable amount of cultural diplomacy resources are dedicated to cultural capacity-building in the developing world.

Infrastructure

- O   154 services for cooperation and cultural activities in embassies
- O   436 cultural institutes abroad (283 are Alliances Française language centres)
- O   Radio France Intérnationale (RFI) boasts 40 million listeners.

New developments

In 2006 'Cultures France' was created – described by Culture Minister Douste-Blazy as a 'British Council à la française'. This will group together a number of national cultural societies and activities.

India

There is increasing awareness of the role of culture in India's rise as a global power, as referenced by PM Manmohan Singh's comments elsewhere in this report.

The major cultural institutions are heavily government controlled, and there is also a specific diplomatic body dedicated to culture – the Indian Council for Cultural Relations (ICCR). Critics suggest that the ICCR prioritises a very traditional representation of Indian culture and cultural activities are carefully vetted in an 'empanelment process' before any support is given. Formal cultural diplomacy is just one aspect contributing to India's rapidly changing profile overseas, although the ICCR currently receives more invitations to feature in cultural programmes than it can deal with. Bollywood, the name given to India's film industry, which spreads far wider than Mumbai and Hindi language films, outsells Hollywood annually by over a billion tickets. But it is not just Bollywood that is reinventing our understanding of India – Indian contemporary art is in demand in the global market as never before. Indian fashion has also 'taken flight' according to a recent *Observer* special issue (70 international buyers were part of India fashion week in October 2006).[74]

Policy home base

The Indian Council for Cultural Relations in Delhi is funded by the Ministry of External Affairs. City governments such as Delhi have also developed international profiles.

Funding

ICCR's approved budget estimates for the year 2004/05 are 5590 lakhs (hundred thousand) Rupees.

Infrastructure

Eighteen ICCR cultural centres abroad, including the Nehru Centre in London, with several more planned, including Washington in the US.

Norway

In recent years, Norway has pursued a more integrated policy of cultural diplomacy. Many of the major organisations involved, including Visit Norway, Innovation Norway and NORAD (the development agency), have consistent typefaces, imagery, and so forth. A glance at www.norway.org.uk/ shows how highly focused and strategic the Norwegian approach is. The distillation of a series of messages about Norway – embodying notions of a clean environment, wilderness, brave explorers like Nansen and hi-tech modern design – combines to enable Norway to punch above its weight in the international arena. Norway has played a notable role as a peace broker and negotiator and has a reputation as a generous aid donor. The country has decided on a limited number of important relationships for its development programme, and sees helping their cultural infrastructure as a major part of building civil society. Norway's relatively recent emergence as a nation – it is only 100 years old – gives it special insights into the infrastructure of national cultural institutions that a new nation might wish to establish.

Policy home base

The Ministry of Foreign Affairs (MFA) is the main player in coordinating cultural diplomacy efforts, and has set three strategic priorities for Norway's embassies: peace and development, natural resources, and 'a modern nation'. Responsibility for cultural relationships in the south is being transferred from the development agency NORAD to the MFA.

Infrastructure

Cultural institutional autonomy is formally maintained and the MFA recognises that policy must go with the grain of cultural aims and practices, but, as they say, 'everyone knows the messages'. The clarity of policy is resented in some quarters as counterproductive. One interviewee said that the relationship is the wrong way around: 'Art is way ahead of politics in re-defining global relationships, identities and collaborations.' The national arts council is Kuturrad, established in 1965 along the lines of the UK model, and there is also an independent national theatre and national gallery.

New developments

Norway uses its distinctive cultural icons in pursuit of foreign policy. For example, 'Ibsen Year' in 2006 involved 8059 separate events across 83 countries from all continents and was constructed around the playwright's themes of corruption, the contemporary and gender equality (which is known in China as 'Norwegianism'). Culture in Norway faces the same issues of measurability as in other countries, although, as the MFA said, 'development issues are long term and unmeasurable'.

The US

The relation between culture and politics in the US is tense. Historically, they have been kept very separate, hence the pre-eminence of private sponsorship for culture and the separation of roles between New York and Washington, where the former is the cultural capital and the latter is the centre of US politics. Culture has come to the fore of international relations in isolated bursts: during the Cold War, the freedom of US culture, embodied in Abstract Expressionism and Jazz, was used to promote American values and undermine those of the USSR. Now, cultural diplomacy has fallen out of use. However, the appeal of US popular culture (from Coca-Cola to Hollywood and Levis) is one of the most potent, but uncontrolled, forces in the cultural world today.

Policy home base

Cultural diplomacy used to be overseen by the USIA but this organisation was disbanded by the Clinton administration in the 1990s. Its responsibilities now sit under the US Department of State. The Smithsonian Institution plays an international role as a cultural hub: although nominally representative of the US (it is functionally and legally a body of the federal government, with eight of its 17 regents being state officials), its component institutions operate with the same freedom as other major institutions, like the Metropolitan Museum of Art in New York.

Funding

There is little tradition of state funding of culture in the US. Culture is not seen as falling within the federal remit and so federal encroachment attendant to funding can be seen with scepticism. Much initiative on the part of institutions is therefore funded by foundations and individual donations, with generous tax arrangements available to incentivise donation.

Infrastructure

O   Major US embassies have cultural attachés.

O   The State Department has assumed some of the responsibilities of the former USIA.

O   The Voice of America reaches an estimated 115 million listeners per week and, in financial year 2006, had a budget of $166 million. It broadcasts in 44 languages and has a clear remit in charter to 'represent America'.

O   Individual artists, performers and others act as 'cultural ambassadors', communicating US cultural forms overseas: Toni Blackman is a 'hip-hop ambassador', and ice skater Michelle Kwan occupies a similar role.

New developments

There is growing awareness that the appeal of US brands is waning. With the growth of tensions in the Middle East, the State Department and others are looking to the success of cultural diplomacy during the Cold War as a precedent, and there is a clear sense that any state-funded cultural diplomacy must be strictly in the national interest. The emphasis is very much on promoting immediate US interests overseas – President Bush appointed his personal friend and former Madison Avenue advertising executive, Karen Hughes, as his Under Secretary of State for Public Diplomacy and Public Affairs.

Notes

1   According to J Nye, see www.foreignaffairs.org/20040501facomment83303/
    joseph-s-nye-jr/the-decline-of-america-s-soft-power.html (accessed 6 Feb
    2007).
2   Laqueur, 'Save public diplomacy'.
3   FCO, *Active Diplomacy for a Changing World*.
4   See www.arts.org.uk/aboutus/ambition.php (accessed 2 Feb 2007).
5   DCMS, *International Strategy Document*.
6   www.culture.gov.uk/what_we_do/Arts/international_arts_policy/china_uk.htm
    (accessed 6 Feb 2007).
7   Foister, *Holbein in England*.
8   From an interview with a director of the Palace Museum conducted by a
    Demos researcher in Beijing, 17 Oct 2006.
9   Arndt, *The First Resort of Kings*.
10 R Menon, quoted in Finn, 'The case for cultural diplomacy'.
11 Interview with Ed Mortimer and Demos researchers, 12 Jul 2006.
12 From the *American Heritage Dictionary of the English Language*, 4th edn, viewed
    at Dictionary.com website (29 Sep 2006), see http://dictionary.reference.com/
    browse/diplomacy (accessed 7 Feb 2007).
13 Nye, *Soft Power*.
14 Leonard, *Public Diplomacy*.
15 For a summary and links to viewing the Carter Review, see www.fco.gov.uk/
    servlet/Front?pagename=OpenMarket/Xcelerate/
    ShowPage&c=Page&cid=1007029395249 (accessed 7 Feb 2007).
16 Leonard, 'Diplomacy by other means'.
17 Interview with Paul de Quincey at British Council Paris, 11 Jul 2006.
18 Wang, 'Localising public diplomacy'.
19 Wolf and Rosen, 'Public diplomacy'.
20 Dyson, 'Reinventing the nation'.
21 See www.fco.gov.uk/Files/kfile/Aichi%20Expo%20Report_1.pdf (accessed 7
    Feb 2007).

22   From FCO, *Active Diplomacy for a Changing World*: (1) making the world safer from global terrorism and weapons of mass destruction; (2) reducing the harm to the UK from international crime, including drug trafficking, people smuggling and money laundering; (3) preventing and resolving conflict through a strong international system; (4) building an effective and globally competitive EU in a secure neighbourhood; (5) supporting the UK economy and business through an open and expanding global economy, science and innovation, and secure energy supplies; (6) achieving climate security by promoting a faster transition to a sustainable, low-carbon global economy; (7) promoting sustainable development and poverty reduction underpinned by human rights, democracy, good governance and protection of the environment; (8) managing migration and combating illegal immigration; (9) delivering high-quality support for British nationals abroad, in normal times and in crises; and (10) ensuring the security and good governance of the UK's Overseas Territories.

23   See www.en.articlesgratuits.com/gastro-diplomacy-101-id411.php (accessed 29 Jan 2007).

24   See http://english.people.com.cn/english/200006/26/eng20000626_43930.html (accessed 6 Feb 2007).

25   Dickie, 'Starbucks faces Forbidden City ban'.

26   See www.youtube.com/t/about (accessed 7 Feb 2007).

27   See http://news.bbc.co.uk/1/hi/entertainment/6230247.stm (accessed 8 Feb 2007).

28   See www.yele.org/vision.html (accessed 8 Feb 2007).

29   See 'China rockin' to Supergirl', *Seattle Times*, 30 Aug 2005, see www.chinadaily.com.cn/english/doc/2005-08/30/content_473432.htm (accessed 15 Jan 2007).

30   See www.publications.parliament.uk/pa/cm200405/ cmselect/cmcumeds/414/41405.htm (accessed 7 Feb 2007).

31   NMDC, *Values and Vision*.

32   See Visit Britain Press Centre, available at www.visitbritain.com/corporate/presscentre/presscentrebritain/pressreleasesov erseasmrkt/jan-mar2006/jan06ips.aspx (accessed 7 Feb 2007).

33   The number of visitors to Alnwick's Tourist Office rose from 65,000 in 2002 to 101,000 in 2003. See www.alnwick.gov.uk/an/webconnect.exe/AO2/View/ ?Version=2986&Site=756&PF=NULL&SiteGroup= (accessed 7 Feb 2007).

34   See Visit Britain Press Centre.

35   *The Art Newspaper* 167 (Mar 2006).

36   See http://seattlepi.nwsource.com/artandlife/1404AP_Art_Louvre.html (accessed 7 Feb 2007).

37   According to Saint Chamas, adviser to the president of the Louvre, the number of Chinese visitors had tripled in the 12 months prior to our interview at the Louvre Museum, Paris, 10 Jul 2006.

38   See www.culture.gov.uk/what_we_do/Creative_industries/ (accessed 7 Feb 2007).

39   DCMS, *International Strategy Document.*
40   Holden and Jones, *Knowledge and Inspiration.*
41   V Westwood, speech at the launch of the Wallace Collection exhibition, *Boucher: Seductive Visions*, 29 Sep 2004.
42   NMDC, *International Dimensions.*
43   Wilsdon and Keeley, *China.*
44   See www.artfund.org/policyandcampaigns/ (accessed 28 Jan 2007).
45   Quoted in Bailey, 'The Metropolitan has 70 times the purchasing power of the British Museum'.
46   See www.rapidimmigration.com/usa/1_eng_info_q1culture.html (accessed 7 Feb 2007).
47   President's Foreword, in Rawski and Rawson (eds), *China.*
48   Rawski and Rawson (eds), *China.*
49   Aspden, 'Cultural exchange'.
50   Logan, 'The revolution will not be satirised'.
51   Portal and McKillop (eds), *North Korean Culture and Society.*
52   See www.discoverislamicart.org (accessed 7 Feb 2007).
53   Mohan, 'India and the balance of power'.
54   PM Manmohan Singh, speech at the *Hindustan Times India* Leadership Summit, New Delhi, Nov 2006.
55   French, 'China witnesses a '70s flashback'.
56   See www.culture.gov.uk/what_we_do/Arts/international_arts_policy/china_uk.htm (accessed 7 Feb 2007).
57   See http://ctc.britishcouncil.org.cn/en/info/index.jsp (accessed 5 Feb 2007).
58   See www.britishcouncil.org/china-arts-artistlinks-whatis.htm (accessed 5 Feb 2007).
59   P Gerstenblith, quoted in Huffstutter and Naji, 'Antiquities stuck in legal limbo'.
60   Ibid.
61   Friedman, *The World is Flat.*
62   Ibid.
63   See, for example, www.nationaltheatre.org.uk/?lid=22114 (accessed 7 Feb 2007).
64   See http://arts.guardian.co.uk/features/story/0,,1925591,00.html (accessed 7 Feb 2007).
65   See www.plantcultures.org.uk (accessed 7 Feb 2007).
66   Elworthy and Rifkind, *Hearts and Minds.*
67   Akbar, *Shamiana.*
68   T Risse, 2000, quoted in Wang, 'Localising public diplomacy'.
69   Arndt, *The First Resort of Kings.*
70   See http://news.bbc.co.uk/1/hi/education/6294643.stm (accessed 7 Feb 2007).
71   See www.prb.org/pdf06/06WorldDataSheet.pdf (accessed 7 Feb 2007).
72   Kynge, *China Shakes the World.*
73   Leonard, *Britain™.*
74   'New India', *Observer Magazine*, 26 Nov 2006.

Bibliography

T Adams, 'The art of subtle diplomacy', *Observer*, 21 May 2006.

S Akbar, *Shamiana: The Mughal tent* (London: V&A Publications, 1999).

S Anholt, *Brand New Justice* (Oxford: Elsevier, 2005).

S Anholt and S Hildreth, *Brand America: The mother of all brands* (London: Cyan, 2004).

H Arero, 'Negotiated spaces: African and UK museums in the 21st century', *ICOM UK Newsletter*, Spring 2006.

R Arndt, *The First Resort of Kings: American cultural diplomacy in the twentieth century* (Dulles, VA: Potomac Books, 2005).

P Askew, *British Library's International Dimension* (London: British Library, 2006).

P Aspden, 'Cultural exchange', *Financial Times Magazine*, 29/30 Oct 2005.

P Aspden, *Selling democracy? The past and future of western cultural relations and public diplomacy* (London: British Council, 2004).

A Asthana, 'British Library sets sights on the East', *Observer*, 23 Apr 2006.

M Bailey, 'Royal Academy to open China show two months early', *The Art Newspaper*, Oct 2005.

M Bailey, 'The Metropolitan has 70 times the purchasing power of the British Museum', *The Art Newspaper* 175 (Dec 2006).

FC Barghoorn, *The Soviet Cultural Offensive: The role of cultural diplomacy in Soviet foreign policy* (Princeton: Princeton University Press, 1960).

K Barysch, C Grant and M Leonard, *Embracing the Dragon: The EU's partnership with China* (London: Centre for European Reform, 2005).

B Benoit, 'Uproar as opera is dropped due to Islamist reprisal fears', *Financial Times*, 26 Sep 2006.

Botanic Gardens Conservation International, *Global Strategy for Plant Conservation*, (London: Secretariat of the Convention on Biological Diversity, 2006).

British Council, *Making a World of Difference: Cultural relations in 2010* (London: British Council, 2006).

British Library, *Annual Report and Accounts* (London: British Library, 2003/04).

British Library, *British Library's Content Strategy: Appendices* (London: British Library, 2006), see www.bl.uk/contentstrategy (accessed 6 Feb 2007).

British Museum Review, *Museum of the World for the World: London, United Kingdom and beyond* (London: British Museum, Apr 2004 to Mar 2006).

C Burgess, C Peila and MJ Wyszomirski, *International Cultural Relations: A multi-country comparison* (Washington, DC: Centre for Arts and Culture, Cultural Diplomacy Research Series, 2003).

H de Burgh, *China: Friend or foe?* (London: Icon, 2006).

O Burkeman, 'Problem with your country's image? Mr Anholt can help', *Guardian*, 11 Nov 2006; see also VisitBritain's website at www.visitbritain.org/britainbrand/britainbrand/BrandOverview.asp (accessed 6 Feb 2007).

D Challis, 'The Parthenon sculptures; emblems of British national security', *British Art Journal* 7, no 1.

A Clarke, L Patten and C Pung, 'Measuring the economic impact of the British Library', *New Review of Academic Librarianship* 10, no 1.

J Cooper Ramo, *Brand China* (London: Foreign Policy Centre, 2006).

L Cox, *Ice Station Antarctica*; Touring Exhibitions Information Pack (London: Natural History Museum, 2005).

L Cox, NHM Art Exhibitions Information Pack (London: Natural History Museum, 2004).

J Craig, *Production Values: Futures for professionalism* (London: Demos, 2006).

Department for Culture, Media and Sport, *International Strategy Document* (London: DCMS, 2006); shared with the authors by consent and viewed online at www.culture.gov.uk (accessed 15 Jan 2007).

Department for Trade and Investment, *Trade and Investment White Paper* (London: UKTI, 2004); shared with the authors by consent.

M Dickie, 'Starbucks faces Forbidden City ban', *Financial Times*, 18 Jan 2007, see www.ft.com/cms/s/a7fadbbe-a6fd-11db-83e4-0000779e2340.html (accessed 8 Feb 2007).

D Dodd, M Lyklema and K Dittrich-van Weringh, *A Cultural Component as an Integral Part of the EU's Foreign Policy?* (Amsterdam: Boekmanstudies, 2006).

L Dyson, 'Reinventing the nation: British heritage and the bicultural settlement in New Zealand' in J Littler and R Naidoo (eds), *The Politics of Heritage: The legacies of race* (London: Routledge, 2005).

S Elworthy and G Rifkind, *Hearts and Minds: Human security approaches to political violence* (London: Demos, 2005).

PM von Eschen, 'Satchmo blows up the world: jazz, race, and empire in the cold war', in R Wagnleitner, *Here, There, and Everywhere: The foreign politics of American popular culture* (Hanover: University Press of New England, 2000).

N Ferguson, *Colossus: The rise and fall of the American empire* (London: Penguin, 2005).

HK Finn, 'The case for cultural diplomacy: engaging foreign audiences', *Foreign Affairs*, Nov/Dec 2003.

S Foister, *Holbein in England*, exhibition catalogue (London: Tate Publications, 2006).

Foreign and Commonwealth Office, *Active Diplomacy for a Changing World: The UK's international priorities* (London: FCO Publications, 2006).

C Frankel, *The Neglected Aspect of Foreign Affairs* (Washington, DC: Brookings Institution, 1965).

H French, 'China witnesses a '70s flashback', *International Herald Tribune*, 9 Dec 2006.

T Friedman, *The World is Flat: The globalised world in the twenty-first century* (London: Penguin, 2006).

J Garreau, 'America, minus a human factor', *Washington Post*, 26 Apr 2006.

A Geddes, 'Migration and the welfare state in Europe' in S Spenser (ed), *The Politics of Migrations* (Oxford: Blackwells, 2003).

J Gittings, *The Changing Face of China: From Mao to market* (Oxford: Oxford University Press, 2005).

S Gregory, 'Anti-US backlash', *Time*, 6 Dec 2004, viewed online at www.time.com/time/magazine/article/0,9171,1009658,00.html (accessed 4 Jan 2007).

J Holden and S Jones, *Knowledge and Inspiration: The democratic face of culture* (London: Demos/Museums, Libraries and Archives Council, 2006).

PJ Huffstutter and K Naji, 'Antiquities stuck in legal limbo', *Los Angeles Times*, 13 Jul 2006.

S Huntington, *The Clash of Civilisations and the Remaking of the World Order* (New York: Simon & Schuster, 1998).

W Hutton, *The Writing on the Wall: China and the West in the 21st century* (London: Little, Brown, 2007).

International Dunhuang Project, *Newsletter of the International Dunhuang Project* (London: IDP, 2005).

Italian Institute of Culture, *Archaeological Sites in Iraq* (Brussels: Italian Institute of Culture, 2003).

J Jiang, 'Found in translation', *Business Weekly*, China Daily, 16 Oct 2006.

J Joffe, 'Who's afraid of Mr Big?' *The National Interest*, Summer 2001.

S Jones, 'The new cultural professionals', in J Craig (ed), *Production Values: Futures for professionalism* (London: Demos, 2006).

S Jones and P Bradwell, *As You Like It* (London: Demos, 2007).

N Klein, *No Logo* (London: Flamingo, 2001).

C Knight, 'Portrait of a cultural battle', *Los Angeles Times*, 4 Apr 2006.

ML Krenn, *Fall-Out Shelters for the Human Spirit: American art and the Cold War* (Chapel Hill, NC and London: University of North Carolina Press, 2005).

R Kurin, *Smithsonian Folklife Festival: Culture of, by and for the people* (Washington, DC: Smithsonian Institution, 1998).

J Kynge, *China Shakes the World* (London: Wiedenfeld and Nicolson, 2006).

W Laqueur, 'Save public diplomacy', *Foreign Affairs* 73, no 5, Sep/Oct 1994.

C Leadbeater, *Britain's Creativity Challenge* (London: Creative and Cultural Skills, 2004), available at www.ccskills.org.uk/publications/index.asp (accessed 6 Feb 2007).

M Leonard, *Britain™* (London: Demos, 1997).

M Leonard, 'Diplomacy by other means', *Foreign Policy*, Sep/Oct 2002.

M Leonard, *Going Public: Diplomacy for the information society* (London: Foreign Policy Centre, 2000).

M Leonard, *Public Diplomacy* (London: Foreign Policy Centre, 2002).

M Leonard and A Small, *British Public Diplomacy in the 'Age of Schisms'* (London: Foreign Policy Centre, 2005).

M Leonard and A Small, *Norwegian Public Diplomacy* (London: Foreign Policy Centre, 2003).

J Littler and R Naidoo (eds), *The Politics of Heritage: The legacies of race* (London: Routledge, 2005).

B Logan, 'The revolution will not be satirised', *Guardian*, G2, 5 Feb 2007.

J Lovegrove (ed), *Travel Trends: A report on the 2005 International Passenger Survey* (London: Office of National Statistics, 2006).

D Lowenthal, 'Heritage wars', *Spiked Culture*, 16 Mar 2006 viewed online at www.spiked-online.com/index.php?/site/article/254/ (accessed 15 Jan 2007).

M Mauss, *The Gift* (London: Routledge, 1990).

R McKenna, A Szántó and M Wise, *Arts and Minds: Cultural diplomacy amid global tensions* (New York: National Arts Journalism Program, Arts International and the Centre for Arts and Culture Publication, 2003).

T Modood, 'Muslims and the politics of difference' in S Spenser (ed), *The Politics of Migrations* (Oxford: Blackwells, 2003).

CR Mohan, 'India and the balance of power', *Foreign Affairs*, Jul/Aug 2006.

Museums, Libraries and Archives Council, *Cultural Spend and Infrastructure: A comparative study* (London: AEA Consulting, 2006).

National History Museum, *Planning and Design Consulting Publication* (London: Natural History Museum, 2006).

National Museum Directors' Conference, *International Dimensions* (London: NMDC, 2002).

National Museum Directors' Conference, *Values and Vision: The contribution of culture* (London: NMDC, July 2006), available at www.nationalmuseums.org.uk/values_and_vision.html (accessed 8 Feb 2007).

B Nichols, 'How rock n' roll freed the world', *USA Today*, 6 Nov 2003.

Norad, *Strategy Towards 2010 Publication* (Oslo: Norwegian Agency for Development Cooperation, May 2006).

Norwegian Ministry of Culture and Church Affairs, *Cultural Policy up to 2014* (Oslo: Kultur-OG Kirkedepartementet, 2002–03).

J Nye, 'The decline of America's soft power', *Foreign Affairs*, May/June 2004, viewed online at www.foreignaffairs.org (accessed 15 Jan 2007).

J Nye, *Soft Power: The means to succeed in world politics* (New York: Public Affairs, 2004).

K Ogoura, 'Cultural diplomacy in the Middle East', *Japan Times*, 19 Jul 2006, viewed online at http://search.japantimes.co.jp/print/eo20060717ko.html (accessed 15 Jan 2007).

M Pachter and C Landry, *Culture at the Crossroads* (Stroud: Comedia, 2001).

D Papademetriou, 'Managing rapid and deep change in the newest age of migration', in S Spenser (ed), *The Politics of Migrations* (Oxford: Blackwells, 2003).

Pew Global Attitudes Project, 'No global warming alarm in the US, China' *15-Nation Pew Global Attitudes Survey* (Washington, DC: Pew Research Centre, Jun 2006).

C Picard, 'Iraqi museum staff to receive training in US', *The Art Newspaper*, Jun 2006.

J Portal and B McKillop (eds), *North Korean Culture and Society*, British Museum Research Papers 151 (London: British Museum, 2004).

E Rawski and J Rawson (eds), *China: The three emperors, 1662–1795*, exhibition catalogue (London: Royal Academy, 2005).

Re:Source: The Council for Museums, Archives and Libraries, *International Activity: A strategic plan for action* (London: *Re*:Source, 2001).

Re:Source: The Council for Museums, Archives and Libraries, *International Activity in English Museums, Archives and Libraries* (London: *Re*:Source, 2003).

Re:Source: The Council for Museums, Archives and Libraries, *International Sources of Funding for Museums, Archives and Libraries* (London: *Re*:Source, 2003).

Re:Source: The Council for Museums, Archives and Libraries, *Mapping the Infrastructure of the Museums, Archives and Libraries Sector in Slovenia* (London: *Re*:Source, 2003).

A Riding, 'Rerun our Cold War cultural diplomacy', *New York Times*, 27 Oct 2005, viewed online at www.nytimes.com/2005/arts/27essa.html (accessed 15 Jan 2007).

N Rosenthal et al, *Sensation: Young British artists from the Saatchi Collection* (London: Thames and Hudson and the Royal Academy of Arts, 1997).

Royal Botanic Gardens Kew, *Corporate Plan* (London: Royal Botanic Gardens Kew Publication, 2006), shared with the authors by consent.

CP Schneider, 'Culture communicates: US diplomacy that works' in J Melissen (ed), *The New Public Diplomacy: Soft power in international relations* (Basingstoke: Palgrave Macmillan, 2005).

C Schneider, *Diplomacy that Works: 'Best practices' in cultural diplomacy* (Washington, DC: Centre for Arts and Culture, Cultural Diplomacy Research Series, 2003).

F Stonor Saunders, *Who Paid the Piper? The CIA and the cultural cold war* (London: Granta, 1999).

H Tuch, *Communicating with the World in the 1990s* (Washington, DC: USIA Alumni Association and The Public Diplomacy Foundation, 1994).

J Wang, 'Localising public diplomacy: the role of sub-national actors in nation branding', *Place Branding* 2, no 1 (2006).

J Wilsdon and J Keeley, *China: The next science superpower?* (London: Demos, 2007).

C Wolf Jr and B Rosen, 'Public diplomacy: how to think about it and improve it', RAND Occasional Paper (Santa Monica, CA: RAND, 2004). See www.rand.org/pubs/occasional_papers/OP134/index.html (accessed 8 Feb 2007).

Organisations interviewed

China

Ai Wei Wei, Artist
The Beijing Botanical Garden
The British Council, China
The British Embassy, Beijing
The Central Party School of CPC, Institute of International Strategic
    Studies
The China Institute of International Studies
The China Reform Forum
The Chinese Academy of Social Sciences
CSM Media Research
The Economist, China
The Long March Gallery, Beijing
mad Architects, Beijing
Ogilvy Public Relations Worldwide, Beijing
The Palace Museum, Beijing
Platform China, Beijing
Renmin University of China, School of International Studies, Beijing
Today Art Museum, Beijing
22Film, Beijing
The Ullens Centre for the Arts, Beijing
Vision Magazine, Beijing

Ethiopia

British Council, Addis Ababa
British Embassy, Ethiopia
The Ethiopian Heritage Trust
The Ministry of Culture
The Ministry of Youth, Sports and Culture
The National Library and Archives of Ethiopia
The National Museum of Ethiopia
Professor Richard Pankhurst
The University of Addis Ababa, Faculty of Science, Ethiopia Flora
    Project
The University of Addis Ababa, Institute of Ethiopian Studies
Zoma Contemporary Arts Centre

France

American Friends of Versailles
British Council, Paris
Institut du Monde Arabe
Institut Français, London
Ministry of Foreign Affairs
Musée du Louvre
Musée du Quai Branly

India

A Advertising (Delhi)
Mr Roysten Abel, Theatre Director (Delhi)
Anokhi, Jaipur Virasat Foundation (Delhi)
Mrs Sushma Bahl (Delhi)
Rita Kapur Chisti (Academic and Textiles Activist) (Delhi)
The Asian Heritage Foundation (Delhi)
British Council, Delhi (Delhi)
British Council, West India (Mumbai)
Chhatrapati Shivaji Maharaj Vastu Sagrahalaya (Mumbai)
Counselage (Delhi)

Cymroza Art Gallery (Mumbai)
DASTKAR, Society for Crafts and Craftspeople (Delhi)
Mr Vikas Dilawari (Conservation Architect) (Mumbai)
DNA Academy (Mumbai)
Entertainment Media Services PVT Ltd (Delhi)
The Financial Times South Asia Bureau (Mumbai)
The Hindustan Times (Mumbai)
The Indian Council for Cultural Relations (Delhi)
Indira Gandhi National Centre for the Arts (Delhi)
INTACH (Delhi)
International Herald Tribune, South Asia correspondent
    (Mumbai)
Isharia Puppet Theatre Trust (Delhi)
Sumant Jayakrishnan (Freelance art director and designer) (Delhi)
Khoj International Artists Association (Delhi)
Lotus Architecture and Design (Delhi)
Maya Entertainment (Mumbai)
Mukta Arts Ltd (Mumbai)
National Gallery for Modern Art (Delhi)
Nature Morte Gallery (Delhi)
Sanskriti Foundation (Delhi)
The School of Planning and Architecture, Urban Design Department
    (Delhi)
Seher, Delhi Government arts adviser (Delhi)
Sony Music, India (Mumbai)
State Government of Maharashtra, Department of Culture
    (Mumbai)
Task Force on Cultural and Creative Industries (Delhi)
Teamwork Films (Delhi)
The Times of India (Delhi)
Ms Bandana Tiwari, Freelance fashion journalist (Mumbai)
TVB School of Habitat Studies (Delhi)
Whistling Woods International Film School (Mumbai)
Zee Cafe, Zee Trendz, Zee Telefilms Ltd (Mumbai)

Norway

ABM Utvikling (Norwegian Archive, Library and Museum
   Authority)
The British Council, Oslo
Kulturrad (Norwegian Arts Council)
The National Museum of Art, Architecture and Design
Norwegian Literature Abroad (NORLA)
Norwegian Ministry for Foreign Affairs, Culture Department

UK

Asia House
BBC Worldwide
The British Council
The British Library
The British Museum
The Cultural Section of the Embassy of the People's Republic of
   China
Department of Culture, Media and Sport
The International Council of Museums (ICOM)
The London Confucius Institute, School of Oriental and African
   Studies
The Museum of London
The Natural History Museum
The Royal Academy of Arts
The Royal Botanic Gardens, Kew
The Royal Opera House
The Runnymede Trust
UK Trade and Investment
The Victoria & Albert Museum

US

The Academy for Educational Development, Washington, DC
The Art Institute of Chicago
BBC, Washington, DC

The British Consulate, Chicago
The British Council, Washington, DC
The British Embassy, Washington, DC
Brookings Institute, Saban Center, Washington, DC
The Carnegie Endowment for International Peace, Washington, DC
The Carnegie Hall, New York
The Cato Institute, Washington, DC
Control Risks, Washington, DC
The Field Museum, Chicago
The Frick Collection, New York
Georgetown University, School of Foreign Service, Public Policy Institute
The German Marshall Fund of the United States
The International Peace Academy
The Library of Congress, Washington, DC
The Metropolitan Museum of Art, New York
The Museum of Modern Art, New York (MoMA)
The Museum of Science and Industry, Chicago
The National Arts Journalism Program, New York
The National Endowment for the Arts, Washington, DC
The National Gallery of Art, Washington, DC
The New America Foundation, Washington, DC
The Pew Global Attitudes Project, Washington, DC
The Pierpont Morgan Library, New York
The Program on International Policy Attitudes
The RAND Corporation, Washington, DC
The Smithsonian Institution, Center for Folklife and Cultural Heritage, Washington, DC
The Smithsonian Institution, National Museum of Natural History, Washington, DC
The Smithsonian Institution, National Portrait Gallery, Washington, DC
The Smithsonian Institution, Office of International Relations, Washington, DC

The United Nations (UN), New York
The United Nations Alliance of Civilisations, New York
University of Colorado at Denver, School of Public Affairs
The US Department of State, Bureau of Educational and Cultural Affairs
The US Institute of Peace, Washington, DC

DEMOS – Licence to Publish

THE WORK (AS DEFINED BELOW) IS PROVIDED UNDER THE TERMS OF THIS LICENCE ("LICENCE"). THE WORK IS PROTECTED BY COPYRIGHT AND/OR OTHER APPLICABLE LAW. ANY USE OF THE WORK OTHER THAN AS AUTHORIZED UNDER THIS LICENCE IS PROHIBITED. BY EXERCISING ANY RIGHTS TO THE WORK PROVIDED HERE, YOU ACCEPT AND AGREE TO BE BOUND BY THE TERMS OF THIS LICENCE. DEMOS GRANTS YOU THE RIGHTS CONTAINED HERE IN CONSIDERATION OF YOUR ACCEPTANCE OF SUCH TERMS AND CONDITIONS.

1. **Definitions**
   a   **"Collective Work"** means a work, such as a periodical issue, anthology or encyclopedia, in which the Work in its entirety in unmodified form, along with a number of other contributions, constituting separate and independent works in themselves, are assembled into a collective whole. A work that constitutes a Collective Work will not be considered a Derivative Work (as defined below) for the purposes of this Licence.
   b   **"Derivative Work"** means a work based upon the Work or upon the Work and other pre-existing works, such as a musical arrangement, dramatization, fictionalization, motion picture version, sound recording, art reproduction, abridgment, condensation, or any other form in which the Work may be recast, transformed, or adapted, except that a work that constitutes a Collective Work or a translation from English into another language will not be considered a Derivative Work for the purpose of this Licence.
   c   **"Licensor"** means the individual or entity that offers the Work under the terms of this Licence.
   d   **"Original Author"** means the individual or entity who created the Work.
   e   **"Work"** means the copyrightable work of authorship offered under the terms of this Licence.
   f   **"You"** means an individual or entity exercising rights under this Licence who has not previously violated the terms of this Licence with respect to the Work, or who has received express permission from DEMOS to exercise rights under this Licence despite a previous violation.

2. **Fair Use Rights.** Nothing in this licence is intended to reduce, limit, or restrict any rights arising from fair use, first sale or other limitations on the exclusive rights of the copyright owner under copyright law or other applicable laws.

3. **Licence Grant.** Subject to the terms and conditions of this Licence, Licensor hereby grants You a worldwide, royalty-free, non-exclusive, perpetual (for the duration of the applicable copyright) licence to exercise the rights in the Work as stated below:
   a   to reproduce the Work, to incorporate the Work into one or more Collective Works, and to reproduce the Work as incorporated in the Collective Works;
   b   to distribute copies or phonorecords of, display publicly, perform publicly, and perform publicly by means of a digital audio transmission the Work including as incorporated in Collective Works;
   The above rights may be exercised in all media and formats whether now known or hereafter devised. The above rights include the right to make such modifications as are technically necessary to exercise the rights in other media and formats. All rights not expressly granted by Licensor are hereby reserved.

4. **Restrictions.** The licence granted in Section 3 above is expressly made subject to and limited by the following restrictions:
   a   You may distribute, publicly display, publicly perform, or publicly digitally perform the Work only under the terms of this Licence, and You must include a copy of, or the Uniform Resource Identifier for, this Licence with every copy or phonorecord of the Work You distribute, publicly display, publicly perform, or publicly digitally perform. You may not offer or impose any terms on the Work that alter or restrict the terms of this Licence or the recipients' exercise of the rights granted hereunder. You may not sublicence the Work. You must keep intact all notices that refer to this Licence and to the disclaimer of warranties. You may not distribute, publicly display, publicly perform, or publicly digitally perform the Work with any technological measures that control access or use of the Work in a manner inconsistent with the terms of this Licence Agreement. The above applies to the Work as incorporated in a Collective Work, but this does not require the Collective Work apart from the Work itself to be made subject to the terms of this Licence. If You create a Collective Work, upon notice from any Licencor You must, to the extent practicable, remove from the Collective Work any reference to such Licensor or the Original Author, as requested.
   b   You may not exercise any of the rights granted to You in Section 3 above in any manner that is primarily intended for or directed toward commercial advantage or private monetary

compensation. The exchange of the Work for other copyrighted works by means of digital file-sharing or otherwise shall not be considered to be intended for or directed toward commercial advantage or private monetary compensation, provided there is no payment of any monetary compensation in connection with the exchange of copyrighted works.

   c   If you distribute, publicly display, publicly perform, or publicly digitally perform the Work or any Collective Works, You must keep intact all copyright notices for the Work and give the Original Author credit reasonable to the medium or means You are utilizing by conveying the name (or pseudonym if applicable) of the Original Author if supplied; the title of the Work if supplied. Such credit may be implemented in any reasonable manner; provided, however, that in the case of a Collective Work, at a minimum such credit will appear where any other comparable authorship credit appears and in a manner at least as prominent as such other comparable authorship credit.

5. Representations, Warranties and Disclaimer

   a   By offering the Work for public release under this Licence, Licensor represents and warrants that, to the best of Licensor's knowledge after reasonable inquiry:

      i   Licensor has secured all rights in the Work necessary to grant the licence rights hereunder and to permit the lawful exercise of the rights granted hereunder without You having any obligation to pay any royalties, compulsory licence fees, residuals or any other payments;

      ii   The Work does not infringe the copyright, trademark, publicity rights, common law rights or any other right of any third party or constitute defamation, invasion of privacy or other tortious injury to any third party.

   b   EXCEPT AS EXPRESSLY STATED IN THIS LICENCE OR OTHERWISE AGREED IN WRITING OR REQUIRED BY APPLICABLE LAW, THE WORK IS LICENCED ON AN "AS IS" BASIS, WITHOUT WARRANTIES OF ANY KIND, EITHER EXPRESS OR IMPLIED INCLUDING, WITHOUT LIMITATION, ANY WARRANTIES REGARDING THE CONTENTS OR ACCURACY OF THE WORK.

6. Limitation on Liability. EXCEPT TO THE EXTENT REQUIRED BY APPLICABLE LAW, AND EXCEPT FOR DAMAGES ARISING FROM LIABILITY TO A THIRD PARTY RESULTING FROM BREACH OF THE WARRANTIES IN SECTION 5, IN NO EVENT WILL LICENSOR BE LIABLE TO YOU ON ANY LEGAL THEORY FOR ANY SPECIAL, INCIDENTAL, CONSEQUENTIAL, PUNITIVE OR EXEMPLARY DAMAGES ARISING OUT OF THIS LICENCE OR THE USE OF THE WORK, EVEN IF LICENSOR HAS BEEN ADVISED OF THE POSSIBILITY OF SUCH DAMAGES.

7. Termination

   a   This Licence and the rights granted hereunder will terminate automatically upon any breach by You of the terms of this Licence. Individuals or entities who have received Collective Works from You under this Licence, however, will not have their licences terminated provided such individuals or entities remain in full compliance with those licences. Sections 1, 2, 5, 6, 7, and 8 will survive any termination of this Licence.

   b   Subject to the above terms and conditions, the licence granted here is perpetual (for the duration of the applicable copyright in the Work). Notwithstanding the above, Licensor reserves the right to release the Work under different licence terms or to stop distributing the Work at any time; provided, however that any such election will not serve to withdraw this Licence (or any other licence that has been, or is required to be, granted under the terms of this Licence), and this Licence will continue in full force and effect unless terminated as stated above.

8. Miscellaneous

   a   Each time You distribute or publicly digitally perform the Work or a Collective Work, DEMOS offers to the recipient a licence to the Work on the same terms and conditions as the licence granted to You under this Licence.

   b   If any provision of this Licence is invalid or unenforceable under applicable law, it shall not affect the validity or enforceability of the remainder of the terms of this Licence, and without further action by the parties to this agreement, such provision shall be reformed to the minimum extent necessary to make such provision valid and enforceable.

   c   No term or provision of this Licence shall be deemed waived and no breach consented to unless such waiver or consent shall be in writing and signed by the party to be charged with such waiver or consent.

   d   This Licence constitutes the entire agreement between the parties with respect to the Work licensed here. There are no understandings, agreements or representations with respect to the Work not specified here. Licensor shall not be bound by any additional provisions that may appear in any communication from You. This Licence may not be modified without the mutual written agreement of DEMOS and You.